"He's either the best spiritual teacher in ... his mind." - Lisa M. H...

"The difference between Allfaaraa and mc ... . spiritual teachers is that Allfaaraa is uniquely focused on the true nature of spiritual reality." - Mel Ve of Freedom Central

"I have known Allfaaraa for a long time. He is a very gifted, amazing being. In this life he has dedicated himself to teaching others. I consider him a valued friend and teacher. No matter where you are at in the journey of life, you can count on his teachings to guide you." - Wendy Adams of Light Waves Radio

"The information Allfaaraa provides is a great gift to this world. He gives us the truth we've waited so long to hear. This is the information that every human being who is capable of understanding should learn. Allfaaraa gives us the Rulebook for God's Game." - Ashaaraa (Andrea Mullaney)

"The truth will always be the truth and those of us who are blessed with understanding have always known this. In my book, Allfaaraa is the top dog, and without his teaching I would not have understood the last piece of the puzzle. Not only that, but I am able to relay the information like never before to people that are coming into my life. Thank you. Keep up the good work." - Altaria

"I've done so much work getting here only to find that I've been avoiding that one thing that is keeping me from coming into balance. The ego! And now it's like starting over. I'm a walking example of how so many spiritual systems are essentially a form of spiritual bypassing; gaining a sense of peace and an impression of development by avoiding the ego rather than addressing it. Lots of systems talk about inclusion...Integral, WDM etc, but this is the only place I've actually found the real deal, and it so doesn't look like what I thought it would." - Helios

"When you read or listen to Allfaaraa you won't be able to listen to other teachers anymore. You will realize (and feel deep inside) that they have it all backwards, or that they only have some parts of the story while he has all of it. I have been with him for eons and I'm still learning." – Siriliel

"After listening to the first Lisa show, I knew that Allfaaraa's teaching was what I needed in order to put the pieces of the 'puzzle' together. I have never missed a show and have listened more than once. Like many others, I have struggled to grasp it all, but I know it is truth!" – Sharon Miller

"I've always trusted myself and my intuition. Then here comes Allfaaraa into my life, and although every word he said was like a memory I had forgotten, he was telling me things about myself I didn't want to know. And I didn't like it! It took me a while to come around and test him with my heart. To test his whole being; everything he taught; the emotions he puts out there. Everything… And it made me both really mad and really reassured when the 'tests' came out correct." – Alaaniel

"Hold on to your seat belt because this is the fast track and we have got the most amazing and aware teacher with us. A word of advice: take everything that is said from Allfaaraa literally if you can, because there is much more to be unraveled as we go on. And remember that the more understanding you acquire the more light you will attain and the more you will grow yourself and Creator. It is fascinating, astonishing, and brilliant." – Amorah

"The first time I heard Allfaaraa speak I had a visceral response in the deepest core of my being to the profound, illuminated truth of the words that he spoke. The wisdom he imparts is unprecedented. The knowledge he shares with unapologetic certainty and clarity stirred a remembering in my soul of just who I am and why I am here in a way that has changed me forever. Allfaaraa didn't just open doors for me, he blew off the roof." – Ankaaraa

THE KEYS TO ASCENSION

KARMA
FREE WILL & REINCARNATION

ALLFAARAA ANTAARAA AMAARAA

AND

SHAWN CLARK

RAISE THE PLANET

WWW.RAISETHEPLANET.COM

Raise The Planet Publishing
Baltimore, MD
Eagle Nest, NM

For More Information Visit:
www.raisetheplanet.com
@raisetheplanet (Twitter)
RaiseThePlanet (Facebook)

Publisher Inquiries:
publisher@raisetheplanet.com

Cover Design: Siriliel Kando Orlay
Additional Design & Editing: Andrea Mullaney (Ashaaraa)
Editing & Proof Reading: Kelly (Ankaaraa)

ISBN (paperback): 978-0-9858564-5-8
ISBN (eBook): 978-0-9858564-1-0

Printed in USA
Signature Book Printing
www.sbpbooks.com

THE UNDERSTANDING OF YOUR SOUL'S PURPOSE

WILL DETERMINE YOUR CONTRIBUTION OF LIGHT

TO THE CREATOR

ALLFAARAA'S PRAYER

I AM THE SOUL

I AM THE LIGHT DIVINE

I AM LOVE. I AM WILL. I AM FIXED DESIGN

I BRING THE CHRIST INTO MY HEART

I BRING THE HOLY SPIRIT INTO MY BODY

I NOW DON THE LIGHT BODY

HOLY FATHER

GIVE ME THE STRENGTH TO OVERCOME

THE VISION TO SEE

AND THE CLARITY TO UNDERSTAND

THANK YOU

THANK YOU

THANK YOU

THE THREE QUESTIONS

WHAT AM I?

YOU ARE A SOUL (SEED)
A FRAGMENT OF YOUR ANGEL OR SPIRIT (TREE) ABOVE IN
THE CELESTIAL REALM, PLACED INTO A FLESH BODY (SOIL)
TO GROW!

* * *

WHAT IS MY PURPOSE?

TO CREATE YOUR SELF (ANGEL/SPIRIT) ABOVE
THROUGH THE FLESH BELOW.

* * *

WHERE AM I GOING?

WHEN YOU ARE FULLY GROWN
YOU WILL RETURN TO WHERE YOU CAME FROM
THE CELESTIAL REALM
TO TAKE THE NEXT STEP!

THIS BOOK WILL EXPLAIN HOW THE PROCESS WORKS
IN DEPTH STEP BY STEP
SO YOU WILL HAVE THE UNDERSTANDING THAT
THE CREATOR WANTS YOU TO HAVE.

TABLE OF CONTENTS

A NOTE ABOUT OUR TEACHING

This book was originally created from live teachings on our online radio show. We have since revised it to include additional material that someone new to us may not have heard before. We have touched on the basics in order to set a foundation for the material; however, if you have additional questions, you may find it beneficial to visit our website.

www.raisetheplanet.com

Many others have been listening and participating with us since we went public in January of 2012 in a series of interviews with Lisa M. Harrison.

You can find most of our previous interviews and radio shows preserved in the archives of various locations like these:

YouTube – www.youtube.com/user/ALLFAARAA1
BlogTalkRadio – www.blogtalkradio.com/allfaaraa-live
WolfSpiritRadio – www.wolfspiritradio.com

You may also refer to our Facebook page "Raise The Planet" or find some snippets of wisdom on our Twitter feed "@raisetheplanet."

Thank you!

ACKNOWLEDGEMENTS

We are deeply thankful for everyone who has participated in this work and continues to do so. We cherish all of those who listen to our interviews and recorded shows, and who ask questions on the website. You are why we are here and why we are doing this.

Firstly we must thank Lisa M. Harrison who took a chance with us when we first went public. If not for Lisa we might not be where we are now.

We also thank Rebecca Jernigan and Mel Ve and Wendy Adams and Path-O-Sages for their interviews and for the private conversations which have been so inspiring and helpful. We thank everyone who has interviewed us.

We are immensely grateful to Uncle Lacy for the amazing gift which helped so much in the initial printing of this book and which will extend our reach further and sooner than we could have expected.

We are amazed by the artistic work of Siriliel Kando Orlay, and we express our heartfelt appreciation for his video productions, book cover art, and radio show banners.

We thank Andrea Mullaney (Ashaaraa) for her additional cover design work, as well as formatting and editing assistance.

We thank Kelly (Ankaaraa) for her extensive help with editing and proofreading. We are lucky to have a published author on the team.

We are thankful for SaaAnaRaa Leigh Redmill and Amorah Fee Redmill who transcribe the original audio for every show. Your skill and speed is unmatched and invaluable.

And we thank you, the reader, for spending some of your precious time with us. May this information bring light to you in ways that you may not yet understand.

PREFACE

Each of us comes to any book or discussion with the idea that we are open to new ideas. We consider ourselves free to decide what is true and what is not. And yet this is not actually the case. Each of us is already, before a single word is uttered, trapped in a cage of existing mental concepts and beliefs. We have already determined "our truth" before the discussion begins, and anything said during the discussion that disagrees with what we already believe to be true, will likely cause immediate rejection. We may act cordial and ask some questions to clarify, but most of the time nearly all of us believe that we already have a good handle on things.

Each of us thinks through a mind. And that mind is more than happy to fill in any gaps in our knowing by simply making something up. Not only that, but it does so without consulting "us." Our negative attitude toward ignorance, which has been partly produced by society at large, contributes to this problem. Instead of admitting what we don't actually know, we allow our mind to fill in the gaps. And we ourselves seek to fill in the gaps by hearing opinion after opinion from others, many of whom are also doing the same thing.

Can you see the web of illusion and misinformation being created? And the sad truth is that we are more comfortable with this confused state of affairs than we would be with simply not knowing.

Who among us is honest enough to stick to only what we actually know, and admit ignorance to everything else? And yet without that honesty, or at least the acknowledgement that we need to be that honest, we are going to be in immediate danger of confusing our existing mental concepts with reality itself. Our imagination gives us an amazing creative ability, but that ability to represent reality with concepts also leaves us at constant risk of *misrepresenting* reality. And this is exactly what we tend to do.

Notice that reality is whatever it is, *as it is*, regardless of our approval or thoughts about it. Thoughts about reality are not reality *as itself*. We assume that we are perceiving reality as it is, and yet what we are actually perceiving is our thoughts about it. We are seeing it as our mind presents it to us, inclusive of our preferences, assumptions, beliefs, biases, cultural programming, and fears.

This challenge affects all of us, not just those who we may deem "asleep" or spiritually unevolved. Atheists are convinced that science has (or will have) all of the possible answers, and religious followers are convinced that their faith has all of the possible answers. But what about those who deem themselves "spiritual"?

Notice how many, on the road to "truth," become pigeon holed into conspiracy theories, or aliens and UFO's, or "nonduality," or past-life regression. Notice how some people will have a single near-death experience, and then proceed to teach and write books as if they have the answers for humanity. New Agers will discover love and light and "nonduality," and then proceed to feel like they have solved the puzzle of the universe. Gurus will have an experience of "oneness" with the universe and then teach that there is no individuality beyond the body.

What is my point with all of this? It is this: Even if Allfaaraa brings you the raw and accurate truth, how will you be able to hear it if it disagrees in some way with what you currently hold dear? Can you be honest enough to admit what you do and don't know, and remain in a state of not-knowing long enough to make a real discovery of something you may have missed? And can you appreciate how difficult this is to do with any new information? Can you appreciate how difficult it truly is to arrive at spiritual truth? Do you know how tricky the mind is? How it prefers some facts to others? How it twists memories and excludes segments of information without consulting "you"?

Can you neither reject nor believe what you hear (or read), and instead look at everything at once in a holistic fashion, being ruthlessly honest with yourself about what you do and do not truly know?

I have made it a point in my journey to not only look far and wide for my answers (as well as within), but to keep everything "on the table" as I do so. In other words, I rejected nothing along the way. I simply kept adding new types of information to my "evidence." I also made it a regular practice to occasionally *reject everything* and see what came back to me, in order to discover what I really knew, and what I couldn't deny.

In summary, I just want to remind you of your mind and how it works. It will enforce its own will. Your mind is not your own the way you think it is. Modern psychology acknowledges that most of what makes up our thinking is actually beneath our conscious awareness. Allfaaraa and I can confirm that there is a spiritual reason for this.

I also want to remind you that reality (meaning all of it, not just this world) is a whole and complete existence of absolutely everything, and it must be explained that way. Nothing can be left out. Nothing can be excluded.

Here are a few important questions to consider for yourself:

- Can you leave all information on the table, so to speak, and keep looking at all of it in a holistic way until all contradictions have been resolved?
- Can you put your existing concepts aside long enough to make a fresh discovery?
- Can you let go of what you *think* you know long enough to determine what you actually know?
- Can you be profoundly and consistently honest with yourself in your search for what is true?

If you have already looked far and wide for your answers like I have, perhaps you will agree with me when I say that Allfaaraa brings it all together like no one else I have ever seen. I had already gathered and assembled most of the pieces on my own, but Allfaaraa was able to show me how they all fit together. I hope you are ready to see what I see.

Shawn Clark
Baltimore, MD
December 2012

WHO IS ALLFAARAA?

Most of humanity gathers their information from the books they have read, the websites they have seen, and the conversations they have had. It comes from their parents and their schools and their culture and their churches and their governments and their news organizations. They seek and they seek, if they have the courage and desire to look at all, but they are almost always seeking outside of themselves.

I do not read or listen or take in any material of a spiritual nature through books or websites humanly inspired. I am very careful not to contaminate my information.

I used to be a teacher of spirituality and a Celestial channel in the 80's, but now I am finely tuned to only two frequencies: Michael the Archangel and Lucifer the Archangel, as well as their higher selves, which are Lord Michael the Christ and Lord Lucifer, who is the God of this World. These are the frequencies that I am tuned to, so I don't need to channel through them any longer. It is a direct connection between them and me.

That is where all of my information comes from. All of it comes from the Celestial realm and from my own direct experiences in this life and the previous 883 lifetimes. No other sources supply my information. You may find this hard to believe, but it is true nonetheless. Your belief is not required. I will let the information speak for itself.

THIS UNIVERSE IS NOT RANDOM

Understand that our universe is not out of control. It knows what it is doing, and what is happening here is not random. There is an organized system and you are a key integral part of it. Everything is connected like little parts in a machine to serve the greater purpose.

I AM

"I AM" Allfaaraa Antaaraa Amaaraa. I am an Angel of God. Actually, I am the fragment or seed/soul/consciousness of the Angel Allfaaraa that exists above the firmament. The "firmament" is the wall around this world separating the physical and Astral realms from the Celestial realm.

I have been aware since before this world was created, approximately 4 billion years ago. I have incarnated in this world 884 times. I know most all of my lifetimes and have gone through them. I have been a teacher since before the Christ was achieved through the flesh.

THE TWO GROUPS OF SPIRIT

In this universe, there are two groups of spirit being grown. In the lower realm (3D/4D, Physical/Astral), *below* the firmament, there are what is called "Tachtoniem" in Hebrew, which means "the beneath" or "the underneath." Those are what you would call "demons." We also have the "Alyoniem," which are those risen above the wall. They are the Angels that exist *above* the firmament in the Celestial realm. Tachtoniem (demons) are Angels that are created through the flesh body; demons that will *become* Angels.

I AM LIKE YOU

I am no different than any of you, and let me explain this to you, because it is critical to knowing who and what you are and where you come from. We all came down here to experience in this world. We came from the Celestial Realm or 5D. But there is also 6D, 7D, 8D, and all exist in the Celestial. So when I say that I am an Angel, *so are you.*

You have an Angel, or watcher, as the Koran says. Every soul has a watcher or Angel. As the Scriptures say, when Christ Michael is speaking to the Hebrews, "When you die you will become like the Angels in Heaven."

So every soul has an Angel, or a God, or an Elohim. Elohim in Hebrew means "Gods." It's the plural of El. Elohim are all basically Angels or Spirits. Your Angel is the Spirit. You, here in this body, are not a Spirit, you are a soul. But we will explain that later.

I AM A TEACHER

Allfaaraa, my Angel, is a teacher above in the Celestial realm, and has done so since I came out of Lucifer, out of Egypt. Previous to that, I was incarnate as an original Angel of Lucifer. That is to say, I was one of those who left their first estate to come to this world, approximately 4 billion years ago.

Above the firmament, in the Celestial, I, Allfaaraa, teach Celestial beings how to incarnate, how to possess their bodies, how to get the most out of their fragments (souls/seeds) and most importantly, how to return to the

Celestial realm. This is what I do in the Celestial, and down here in this 3D realm I teach Angels and demons incarnate within the flesh body (humanity).

I read nothing written by man. Nothing comes from books. The only books that I do read are the Bible, both the Old Testament and the New Testament, all the Gnostic Scriptures, the Apocrypha, the Dead Sea Scrolls, the Nag Hammadi, and anything Divinely inspired, but nothing written by man.

However, I was prompted about 4 years ago to read Eckhart Tolle's book where he did his work on the ego (pain body), and it was tremendous. I was actually shocked that he even knew what he knew about the ego. I asked both Lucifer and Michael, "How does he know that? It's amazing."

However, what he wrote is the tip of the iceberg, the absolute tip of the iceberg. Tolle uncovered the ego/demon, but that is as far as he got. We begin where Tolle left off. I am going to tell you in a minute about the biggest scam ever! The wool has been pulled over your eyes! But we have to start with some basics first.

ALLFAARAA
Eagle Nest, NM
February 2013

"EGO UP"
VS
"SPIRIT DOWN"

The direction and perspective from which information and truth flows is important.

Most esoteric spiritual teachers take the "ego up" perspective. What does this mean? It means that they perceive through their egos, but they have a little more of the veil removed than the average person. This insight gives them the ability to perceive a higher knowledge of our existence than the 3D mind normally allows.

However, where are they looking? Most are looking into 4D, the Astral reality (and it's only the tip of the illusory Astral iceberg) where they think they have found all there is to know.

These teachers feel that they are "awake" because they are peering beyond 3D. Many of them see the patterns and the manipulation, the alien beings, etc. and they teach that we live in a "manipulated" reality. They *think* they have found the whole truth.

These teachers are looking from the wrong direction. They are perceiving reality from the "ego up" perspective, as if life is all about us, the human egos down here. And it's complicated and confusing as we move through the 4D Astral illusions, seeking and seeking, like peeling an onion one layer at a time.

Do you realize how long it would take to make it through all of the relative "truths" to get to the only truth that really matters for us, in the Celestial? Why is the Celestial important? Because that is where you came from and where you are ascending and returning to.

So why learn through these confusing bits and pieces? Who cares how the matrix of this reality works, if we are not taught why it's here to begin with and what it really means?

Allfaaraa's teachings cut out the 4D Astral "mish mash" and get directly to the Celestial and how it affects us here in this world. Allfaaraa teaches "Spirit down." He explains the mechanics in the Celestial realm and how they apply to us here on Earth. Everything comes "up" to God's Truth in the end anyway.

The workings of this reality are here to facilitate our physical experience and our soul's purpose. You can spend your whole life reverse engineering the matrix, and at the end find out that it has always been perfect the way it is.

The answer is simple. What we seek is ourselves. We are fragments of our Angels above the firmament. We are here to grow God and our Angels. If our Angels are stars, then we create the spiritual material to build those stars and all universes!

We are tiny fragments of great, great beings, and we are here to do great, great work. The rest falls into place once this is truly understood.

Ashaaraa (Andrea Mullaney)
Angel, Student & Editor

INTRODUCTION

This book is about the keys to ascension: karma, free will and reincarnation. These are the three main elements in what we call "the game of God."

As we proceed, however, you will see that this book is about much more than just any one subject. We start with answers to some of the most profound and difficult questions of human existence. Despite the apparent enormity of these questions, they are actually quite basic to the discussion, and the answers are quite simple.

But don't let the simplicity fool you. While some of the answers may be simple, the game of God in this world is anything but. And simplicity can be a stumbling block for the mind that likes something complicated to chew on. Paradoxically, the more simple something is, the harder it can be to fully grasp. We tend to overlook the simple and the obvious.

You may be asking yourself, for instance, why you need to know about something as apparently simple as karma. You may think that you already know what karma is and how it works. You have already heard from spiritual teachers about karma. Maybe you have some idea in your head that makes sense to you. Or maybe you think karma doesn't exist at all.

But as you read further you will find that while karma itself is relatively simple (although usually misunderstood), there are other aspects of our existence here that are not. And the big picture, which includes karma, contains such depth that it will take many books to do it justice. We are simply using the subject of karma to begin explaining that larger picture, which is the "science of God."

THE REPETITION IS ON PURPOSE

You will find that some of the book comes across as repetitive as we approach the same question from several angles or give the same answer in more than one way. This is because of how the mind works. You may have to hear the same thing ten times in five different ways before you realize what it means and why we are saying it.

IMPORTANT QUESTIONS

We start in this book to detail out some of the most important questions of our existence. What is God? Who are we? Where do we come from? Why are we here? Where are we going? How does the system work here? Do we have any choice in the matter? Why do we have an ego? What is an ego? And on and on the questions and answers go.

WE GIVE THE HOW AND THE WHY

While this book is certainly about much more than just karma, we will center the main discussion mostly on karma so that we can bring out every detail of how karma itself works, while simultaneously explaining the peripheral concepts that are needed to understand the whole system. We will not simply tell you something, but we will lay out *why* it is that way. We will give you the mechanics of it and some of the history behind it so you can see it for yourself.

Everything that Allfaaraa teaches comes straight from God, either through Michael or through Lucifer. This way you, the reader, get both sides of the picture. As the truth of God comes through Allfaaraa to you, so does a complete explanation of the information. There is no stone unturned. Allfaaraa will answer and explain each and every question until the student fully understands and has no more questions.

Allfaaraa actually makes God make sense. No longer are we, humanity, subject to the statement, "God works in mysterious ways." Allfaaraa explains all of those mysteries. No longer will God be a mystery to you.

THE SIMPLE TRUTH

Allfaaraa is committed to simplifying the impossible to understand esoteric teachings of the Creator, so that they can be understood through the human mind or ego.

"If you can't explain it simply, you don't know it well enough." - Albert Einstein

This book is the first in a series. Each will be on a topic like walk-ins, the ego, the Bible, or something else. And with each one we will dig deeper into the mysteries of terrestrial existence and the Celestial truths of why we are here.

As we said, this book is about karma, free will, incarnation, and reincarnation. But before we get to those, we need to explain some introductory concepts, like what God is, and why we are here. We will also give a brief explanation of what you are, what this world is, why we incarnate, what a "walk-in" is, how basic numerology works, etc. These will give you a basis for the conversation that follows.

RESPECT THE BASICS

If you speak to professional athletes and ask them about amateurs in their sport, they will say that one of the main differences between amateurs and professionals is that the professionals respect and concentrate on the basics. They know that it is the basics that form the foundation for the rest of the talent and skills that follow. But amateurs are always forgetting the basics, seeing them as boring, and instead playing with complicated flashy tricks and cheats that they think will magically transform them into pros.

Try not to miss what may appear at times to be simple basics. It is the basics that you need to see clearly first. Without that simple foundation, the rest will just become confusing. If the foundation is faulty, then the entire understanding will be wrong. You simply must know and fully appreciate certain aspects of existence up front, or you will have wasted your time with the flashy details.

Now, let's start with the most basic truth of all. It is the most basic and yet, paradoxically, also the "highest."

What is God?

WHAT IS GOD?

Before we talk about why we are here we must explain something very critical to understanding everything else. Although in our teachings we use the word "God" in at least three different ways, in this case we mean God the Creator. The All in All. The meaning that most people are thinking of when they say "God."

So, what is God? Simply put, God is all there is.

GOD IS ALL THERE IS.

There is nothing else in existence. There is nothing that is not "him" (or "her" or "it"). There is no particle, no place, no space, no spirit, no nothing that can be outside of Reality Itself. The Whole. The Source. Whatever name you prefer for him/her/it. Choose whatever name you like, but whomever or whatever *it* is must comprise the whole and complete of everything that exists, visible and invisible, tangible and intangible, good and evil, light and dark.

Later in the book we mention duality, the idea that separation can exist. We explain that when it comes to us and God, this is simply not possible, nor can it be, nor will it ever be. The Creator (God) places himself (you) within himself (your body) in order to grow and awaken himself. You are in him and he is in you. There can be no separation. *God is all there is.*

There is only one place that the Creator can create, and only one substance that he/she can use. He must create within himself, and he must use himself as the substance.

You are inside God, and you probably don't even know it. You always have been, and you always will be. There is no other place you can be. You have never left. It only appears so because of your reduced vibration and the veil, which is your mind.

Whether you are reading this book on paper or an electronic screen, it is God. Your body is God. The ground under your feet is God. The air you breathe is God. There is nothing in existence that is not God-stuff. And this goes for any and all realms of existence. All is energy, all is consciousness, and all is God the Creator. One more time, just to be sure: *God is all there is.*

Understanding this is primary and critical to grasping the how and the why about our reality, and why we are here, and how things work in this universe.

WHAT ARE YOU?

The truth of what you are is very simple, and yet it is unknown to most of humanity.

It may be easier to start with what you are not. You are not the body. The body is a vehicle for your lofty task here. The body is like a car or a house or what you might call an Earth-suit. The body is created from the Earth and with the Earth it will stay. You create it and use it as long as it lasts to serve you, and then you leave it behind and move on. The idea and the awareness that you are the body is an illusion. An illusion created by your mind so that you will play the game of God.

What you are is a seed. A soul. A fragment of a Spirit. And you are here to grow and become. You grow spiritually when you overcome the darkness (drama, evil, etc.) that you have created. You create the darkness and you overcome it.

What is a "seed"? Why do we call you that? Because you are a fragment of a larger Spirit that we call an Angel. The Angel can be considered a "tree." You are a seed dropped from that tree into the "soil," which is your body. Trees drop seeds into soil. Easy and simple. Angels drop souls, smaller fragments of themselves, into bodies.

Angels exist in the Celestial realm, but they also have a physical body which is visible to us here. From our perspective these appear as *stars*. You are a fragment of a star, and that is where the New Age term Star Seed came from. All are actually Star Seeds, not just a select few. You are a Star Seed, the seed of a star or Angel.

In order to experience here you had to reduce your size and vibration until you could fit into a flesh body. This is where the term "fall" came from. You are "fallen" from above, from the Celestial realm of a much higher vibration. Yet, you are not fallen at all. It was a choice, not an accident.

A fragment of a Spirit/Angel is like a seed, but it can also be thought of like a piece of a hologram. Holograms have the unique property of containing the information from the original even when broken into smaller pieces. The smaller pieces simply have a reduced "resolution." But each piece is capable of reconstructing (or becoming like) the original.

Notice that seeds and holograms share a similar property. They both contain all of the information (the blueprint) from the original of which they came, yet in a smaller package. Likewise, you share the blueprint of your Creator, and you similarly have the ability to *become* like the one from which you came.

This is also why we are called "children of God" and why God is sometimes called "Father" or "Mother." Like children, we are simply smaller versions of our "parents" or Creator, and we have the ability to become like them.

So what are you again?

You are a soul, a fragment of your Solar Angel, the star that you are, experiencing and growing in a 3D flesh body.

WHY ARE YOU HERE?

We said in the previous chapter that you are a seed, or soul, fragmented from an Angel, which can be considered a "tree." What do the seeds from trees do? They grow into trees themselves. They grow until they are mature enough to drop seeds of their own.

You (seed/soul) will, hopefully, grow to become a tree, or Angel, yourself. This is your purpose and why you are here. You are growing yourself above (your Angel) through incarnation in the flesh below (your body). You, the soul, are the consciousness of your Angel experiencing in form.

The reason you are here is actually quite simple. You are here to grow and become. You are here *to grow yourself above through the flesh below.*

As a fragment of God, your purpose is just a reduced version of God's purpose. God grows through the growth of his parts. You, being a part of God, grow God by growing yourself. Through your growth, God grows also. And how do you grow? Through the process of bringing light to darkness, which we will describe later.

You grow God by growing yourself. That is why you are here. That is your lofty task that you have chosen. You are here to *become.* There is no other secret or special purpose for which you came here. Until this is accomplished, you have no other primary purpose, mission, or secret agenda.

WHAT IS THIS WORLD?

The world that we all exist in right now was created approximately four billion years ago to grow the Creator through growing ourselves, as we just mentioned.

By "grow" we mean spiritually, not physically. This world was created specifically to grow the Creator (God) and you, and it is the only one of its kind in all of the universes. The reason you came here specifically from other realms is because this place is the only one of its kind. We came here *to grow ourselves above through the flesh below.*

Everyone asked to come here. Whether your life is terrible and full of suffering, or enjoyable and loads of fun, know that you volunteered for it. It was a choice.

This world was specifically created to grow the Creator through the physical forms. We started billions of years ago with worms, with bugs, with dinosaurs, with birds, with "monkey man" and other pre-hominids, until we got to what we call our "Adam." Many different groups participated in this. Yes, there were Annunaki involved at that time, and many other Extra-Terrestrial races, but no longer.

THE FIRMAMENT

What happened is that it got to the point where what we will call the "War in Heaven," spilled down to the Earth. After most all of the defilers of the light were driven off of the planet, there was a cleansing period of the soil. Then, between 5,500 and 8,000 years ago, the Creator restructured the Universe; in fact restructured this "world," and placed a wall around it. You can find this in Genesis 1:1. It is called a "firmament" or, in Hebrew, it is a "Rakia" or wall. There is a wall around this 3D World where nothing can go up, and nothing can come in, except Christ, who passes through, and Lucifer, who used to be able to pass through.

This wall surrounds the Earth, and it extends out past the Pleiades, Sirius, and Orion. Most importantly, the Astral realm is also included, which is the storage area where all spirit or light grown on the planet is stored. The Astral is also where souls go between lives, and what is typically reported through near-death experiences and past-life regression, as well as OBE (out-of-body experience, also called Astral Projection). All souls have an Astral Body which is used to travel and exist in the Astral realm, just like a physical body is used to exist in this physical realm.

Some people believe there is a threat of aliens coming here to "get you" or invade. This is false and untrue. Nothing can come in, and nothing can go out, unless it can pass through the firmament, and only Christ can pass up and down.

THE ORIGINAL LIGHT BEARER

Since the creation of this world and the time when the wall was put into place, all spirit placed into form came through Lucifer. Lucifer was the Light Bearer. Every bit of spiritual material (souls and Spirits) was distributed through Lucifer. He/she was the only source.

Lucifer was the God Maker. You will also notice this in Genesis where the entity associated with the Tree of the Knowledge of Good and Evil, which was Lucifer, said that if they partake of his/her "fruit," that their eyes would be opened and they would be "like Gods," knowing both good and evil.

Lucifer was the first son, first Logos, or first Christ, if you will. He/she was the very first direct fragment of the Creator.

The first time souls were fragmented and placed directly into form from the Creator was at Mount Sinai. They were placed into the bodies of the Hebrews, but we will speak more about that later.

CAUSE AND EFFECT

The Creator's system for growth is cause–and–effect based. *What is caused in the flesh has its effect in the spirit.* You can also say that out of darkness (matter or flesh) comes light (spirit). In this world, darkness governs the growing and refining of light or spirit.

GOD'S BUSINESS

So, what is this world? This world is God's factory or farm. It was designed to increase God by growing his parts. It also feeds the Spirits/Angels and the entire creation in the Celestial realm. In this way it is much like a business. It is a business where the product and the currency are both *spirit*.

WHAT IS THE "EGO"?

We already said that you are a seed or soul, but you are actually two seeds or souls, both in the same body. One is a fragment of your Angel above the firmament and is attached to the heart center. The other comes from the Earth Consciousness and is placed in your crown chakra as your mind. Both are technically souls, but the one in the heart center, which is passive, we call the "soul." The other one, which manifests as your thinking mind, we call the "ego." The ego is active and the soul is passive.

NOT THE STANDARD DEFINITION

Here we need to stop and make a very important distinction that is often misunderstood. By "ego" we do *not* mean the standard definition as used by modern psychology. We also do not mean your human personality in this one life, although the ego is responsible for causing you to believe that you are the body and the personality.

The ego, as we use the term, contains all of the memories of all of your lifetimes, including this one. It is more like the subconscious mind as described by modern psychology, except that the ego also *includes* your conscious mind and personality. It is a specific memory-containing individual aspect of consciousness that extends beyond your awareness of this one life.

The ego is what can be regressed through hypnosis. It is the ego which remembers past lives. You will notice that the ego is accessed through the mind (hypnosis), as opposed to the soul, which can be more directly experienced when the mind is silent (meditation). Notice that, without the memories of the ego, experiences of the soul are reported with phrases like "no self" and "pure consciousness."

EARTH-BASED CONSCIOUSNESS

The ego is the Earth-based consciousness which creates the darkness that the soul must overcome with light. The ego is active and the bringer of darkness and drama. The soul is passive and the bringer of light. The ego is the veil which keeps you from your past-life memories and larger self. It is also the creator and enforcer of the illusion that you are the body. This could not be experienced without the ego. You are not the body. You are that which occupies the body. The ego is actively creating the illusion that you are the body. This is part of its purpose and "job description." The ego is doing exactly what it is meant to do, and yet this is what must be overcome.

The ego anchors and creates the darkness. The soul anchors and brings the light to balance that darkness. Light comes through your Angel and soul.

The darkness created by the ego can be thought of as the resistance that the soul must overcome. Just as muscles need resistance in order to grow, so does your soul. As your ego creates drama and chaos and other forms of darkness, your soul must step in to match them with light so that they can be overcome. When this happens, both ego and soul are grown. You grow yourself by overcoming the darkness which you have created. The ego is your mind. You have no mind of your own. All thought and thereby all action, come through it. "You" are not you.

LIGHT AND DARK

By darkness we mean ignorance, unconsciousness, evil, drama, etc. By light we mean awareness, goodness, peace, understanding, love, etc. Light is also Presence, as in the Presence of God. It can also be said that matter is darkness and spirit is light.

DARKNESS FIRST

In creating darkness first and then balancing it with light, you grow. Darkness then light. Darkness then light. It is very similar to how we make mistakes and then learn from them, or create chaos and then bring order to it.

DOUBLE-MINDED

The system here has been set up by God so that the ego first creates darkness and then the soul brings light to offset and balance it. 2 Corinthians 4:6 – "For God commanded the light to shine out of darkness." This is the system and this is why there is always a tension inside of each person. The Bible calls this being "double-minded."

Indeed, we have two minds. We have one in the head that we call "the mind." This is the ego. But we have another one, in the heart center, which is the "soul," that we call the "Mind of God." This other Mind, the soul, speaks to us through deep, silent feelings and is the only "sense" not controlled by the ego. This is what people call the sixth sense or intuition or conscience.

OPPOSITE PURPOSES

Ego and soul have opposite purposes, and yet their purposes align to ultimately ensure your ascension. The ego ascends through darkness, and the soul ascends through light. Yet those opposing purposes serve one larger purpose. They are like the opposite poles of a battery which drive a single electrical system in a car. Individually they oppose each other, but they ultimately serve the same goal. In the case of the ego and the soul, that goal is ascension and growth for both "you" and the Creator (God).

THE ROYAL SCAM

I call it *the greatest truth you can never grasp*. I also call it "the royal scam." If you find this chapter easy to accept, then you are either very advanced spiritually or you are kidding yourself. I might as well just come out and say it.

Your mind is not your own.

Yes, that's what I said. You think through it, and it controls your thoughts, emotions, and actions. The mind that you live and think through is really another soul that lives inside the flesh body. We began to discuss it in the last chapter, but we left out the really difficult part. We explained that it anchors and creates the darkness, and that it records and holds your memories, but we did not elaborate yet on the whole truth of what it means to have an ego as we define it.

The ego acts as your mind or primary consciousness, but it is not you! This mind/soul enforces the illusion that you are human and this body. It is fragmented from the Earth Consciousness. You can call that entity "Gaia," you can call it "Lucifer," you can call it the "Spirit of Error," as it is addressed in the Gnostic Scriptures and Gospels, or you can call it the "Spirit of the World," as the Bible addresses it.

This fragment acts as your mind. You think through a larger being. Your mind is not your own. I know this is a heavy statement, because you believe that you are human, and that you are this body, but you are not.

THE ANCHOR OF THE DARKNESS

This mind we call the "ego." I also refer to it as the "demon" or the "demoness," which refers to its role as the anchor of the darkness. The individual ego anchors the individual darkness the same way that Lucifer anchors the planetary darkness. Tolle calls it the ego and pain body. In our work the pain body is actually the demon/demoness or soul that grows.

When this was first revealed to me in 2004 in a direct teaching with Lucifer in a tiny little room up in the mountains, he unveiled my mind so that I could see. I said, "Oh my God, you live in us." "Yes" was the answer. "Oh my God, I am thinking through you. Are you going to kill me now?" I wet my pants shaking from the fear of knowing what no one knows. "What's next?" I wondered.

It was so enormous. Even with all I had known, I had never known this. But I had always felt there was something else. Something didn't make sense. Lucifer then led me to the proof in writing. There were several verses in Scripture that he/she directed me to read.

Romans 7:17-21 – "Now it is no more that I do it, but 'sin' that dwells within me. For I know that in me, that is in my flesh, dwells no good thing. Now if I do that which I would not, it is no more I that do it, but sin that dwells in me. When I would do good, evil is present with me."

James 4:5, 7&8 – "Do you think that the scripture says in vain the spirit that dwells in us lusts to envy? Resist the devil and he will flee from you. Cleanse your hands you sinners and purify your hearts you double-minded."

2 Thessalonians 2:3&4 – "And that creature of sin be revealed, the son of perdition. Who opposes and exalts himself above all that is called God or that is worshipped, so that he, as God, sits in the temple of God, showing that he is God."

What is the temple of God? You are! Evil lives in you as the fragment of Lucifer, which we call the "ego."

1 Corinthians 3:16 – "Know you not that you are the temple of God and that the Spirit of God dwells in you."

THEY WON'T BELIEVE YOU ANYWAY

After reading the Scripture that I was directed to read, I felt comforted. "Alright," I thought, "the secret had been disclosed a long time ago, yet no one understood." I asked Lucifer, "Can I tell humanity about this? Can I tell them the whole truth?" He said, "Go ahead little Allfaaraa. Tell them. They won't believe you anyway. They can't and they won't." And then there was this big laugh. I fell down on the bed and slept for two days, afraid to wake up. But I did wake eventually, and the teachings continued as if nothing had happened. But I knew. I felt it. I knew as I had always known. There was something inside of me controlling everything I did.

I have struggled to teach about the ego/mind that is not your own. Sometimes it had seemed pointless to even try. However, in the last year, I have finally succeeded in teaching a small group of people who have become familiar with our work. This group of students has come to the truth and finally knows that there is another consciousness, not their own; a mind that lives in them and controls everything. I call it the "ego." It is a soul and it acts as their mind. But it is not "theirs," meaning they are not in full control of it. It creates and forces their choices. These students have proven it to themselves, and they know, indeed, that the mind they think through is not their own.

They can tell you that their mind is not their own. They are thinking through a larger being. They have observed this being in action causing drama and darkness over and over. They have been establishing a loving relationship with this being as they have come to realize that he/she is the driving force in their ascension or return to the Celestial realm.

THERE ARE TWO OF YOU

Again, remember, you are not the body. You are that which inhabits the body, and there are two of you. There is the soul connected to the heart center, which is the fragment or aspect of your Angel, your God, call it whatever you want. And there is the soul/fragment of the Earth Consciousness that acts as your mind that you think through. It is the "god of you" and it controls all of your senses. The only thing it does not control is the "feeling" from the heart center (not to be confused with emotions, which are created by thought). This soul (which we call the "ego") governs your growth process, spiritually speaking. It governs your ascension process.

You came here as a tiny little seed. You came here to create yourself above through the flesh below. The ego/mind, or fragment of the Earth Consciousness, governs the creation of you and God, yet you have not known this, nor could you. Your mind has kept you in slavery. You are a slave to the game of God, growing light through darkness, reincarnating over and over and over.

But do not think it is without purpose. This universe knows what it is doing. Everything has one purpose and one cause. This universe is cause and effect based. What is caused in the flesh has its effect in the spirit. The ascension process goes upward, from soul to Angel to Archangel to Lord to Christ all the way up to the Creator. You are a fragment of the entire creation and you came here *to create yourself above through the flesh below.*

SOUL MATES

Some people speak about soul mates. The truth is that *you are your own soul mate.* You are a soul, and your mate is a soul. That means no body elementals, no hobbits, no tree fairies, and no animal totems.

A soul mate is a soul, and most all of humanity has been seeking that *outside* of themselves. They think their soul mate is another person, but *you* are the soul that you have been seeking. Your other half is the ego, the soul and fragment of the Earth Consciousness.

For you to ascend and return, it (the ego) has to come with you. Both ego and soul will be merged through your heart center. When these two fragments are merged they will become one new Spirit, Angel, or God (all names for the same thing).

MEMORIES

All of the memories of whom and what you have been in every incarnation and every experience are contained within the ego, the mind that you think through. Without your memories there is no "you." Consider it. As a being of consciousness your identity is wrapped up in your memory. You are the totality of everything you have experienced. If you return without your memories (ego) there will be no "you" when you get there. What kind of Angel would you be if you didn't know who you were and retain your prior experiences? How would you create your own realm without knowing how to do so, and without a Self to give to that realm?

THE EGO ASCENDS TOO

The purpose of the ego is to ascend also, just like your soul's purpose. Ascension really is just a return. Remember, we came from above the wall. We began as a little tiny seed, as a little tiny fragment of our Divine Self. We came from there, so ascension is just a return home. But to do it we have to grow. We must match the light (maturity) of the Celestial realm.

The soul's first purpose is to grow itself (you). In growing yourself, you grow the Creator, the All in All. You are a little piece, and as the pieces get bigger the whole gets bigger also.

THE CREATOR'S PLAN

Let me tell you what the Creator's plan is. Not only do I

know first hand, but after teaching me for years they then showed me in print. They would take me to either the Scriptures or the Gnostic Gospels or the Dead Sea Scrolls, and again it was all in there.

I would say, "Wow, first you taught me and I didn't believe it (because some of this stuff was so out there), but then I saw it in print." I didn't read it and then ask. They taught me first, and then they validated it in writing.

One of the things they took me straight to was Ephesians 1, 9 and 10. Christians don't know this. When I used to bring this verse up, when I used to debate with them, they would say "Huh, what?" And I would say, "It is right in your book, but you don't know what it means."

Ephesians 1:9 & 10 – "Having made known unto us the mystery of his will, that in the fullness of time he might gather together in one, all things in Christ, both which are in Heaven and on Earth."

This is Gods plan, to merge Heaven and Earth, through Christ in you. That is the plan. To put all of the Spirit above into all of the matter below (your body), through Christ (in your heart center).

YOU ARE A SLAVE TO THE EGO

So we discussed that God the Creator is All in All. There is no duality because nothing is separated from God. Everything is created of him and by him. Your very body is him also. Whether you are creating (or expanding) light or darkness, you are growing the Creator. Good and evil are both the Creator. He is all things.

However, before you can do anything by choice, you must have complete control of "you." Otherwise, as I have said, you are a slave to the grind. Before you can do anything, you must know who you are, why you are here, what you are here to do, and how you do it. Your ego, or mind, which enforces the illusion that you are this body and that you are human, has you enslaved. Remember, you are not human. You are the fragment of the Spirit that has been growing through each incarnation within the human body.

"YOU" ARE NOT YOU

Your ego/mind that you think through controls everything that you do and keeps you enslaved to the system. They say that "we" only use about 10% of our brain. That's because the other 90% is used by the ego, and it controls all of your senses and most all of your thinking and reacting to life's situations.

Now understand this: what is "your truth"? Where does it come from? It is the totality of all of your experiences, every experience you have. And I mean in this lifetime only, because you are veiled to your past ones. The ego/mind, or fragment of the Earth Consciousness, is the veil. It is the veil to your memories and your larger self. And you are veiled so that you play God's game.

What you think you are is the totality of every experience that you have had in this incarnation. This includes everything you have seen and heard and read in books. It is everything that your ego has assembled to create what you are in your mind, and every physical life experience. This is the "you" that you *think* you are. And it is false! It is the illusion that keeps you in bondage. In short, "you" are not you. In order to be yourself you must *know* your self, your *whole* self.

As one of my great students said recently, "You are like a self-made pizza. You apply whatever 'toppings' that you prefer, and the toppings are like your understanding. Piece by piece you grab whatever you like to assemble 'your truth.' But your truth is not necessarily *the* truth."

THE PERSONALITY

The ego created the personality, everything that you *think* you are. It is called an "inner personality" that the ego has developed for you. It creates the personality, and it keeps your awareness limited to the personality. But you are much more than just the personality of this single life. You are all of your lives combined, plus the God Self from which you have come.

HOW THE EGO MANIPULATES YOU

The ego uses the *past* to enforce its will in the present, to manipulate and control everything. It uses past memories to affect present outcomes, ensuring that darkness will be generated almost always, even if only in thought.

It also uses worry and other types of fear about the *future*. You have to understand the power that the ego maintains. It controls all five senses and your thinking. This is why I call it "the god of you." It can bring you to your knees by pushing the fear button. This is why you must overcome your fears and you must know that you are not the body.

Some of you may have experienced fear just from reading this. That is your ego trying to get you to look the other way. It does not want to be discovered. Darkness is skilled at remaining hidden. In fact, darkness can only exist as long as it is hidden or misunderstood (not seen for what it is). The moment it is seen clearly, it loses power over you. Even after being caught, it regains that power by removing your memory of it. Seeing the truth is one thing. Remembering it is another.

THE EGO CREATES YOUR KARMA

Understanding the ego (and witnessing it in action) is paramount in overcoming it. It is also an important aspect of the discussion about karma because it is the ego which makes the choices which incur karma. It is also the ego which suffers the pain of balancing karma.

The ego is, and always will be, one of the most difficult subjects we ever speak about. This is because everything you think and believe must come through the ego/mind. It controls everything except the deep silent feelings in the heart center.

It can never be overcome. Yet it can be loved into your greatest friend and asset. It can be caught. You can become aware of it. If we have done it, so can you.

WHAT ABOUT EVIL AND DARKESS?

Most of us have a problem with evil and darkness, so we might as well address it here. We assume, whether consciously or unconsciously, that these are somehow a mistake. That they crept into the universe (or this planet) unnoticed, and cannot possibly be part of the plan, and might even be out of control somehow. "Certainly our God is a good God," most would say. Let's look at a verse from the Bible that addresses this. It is God speaking in the first person.

Isaiah 45:7 - "I am the light and I am the dark. I make peace and I create evil."

God is the light, and God is the dark. Whether darkness is increased or light is increased, God is increased.

If *God is all there is*, then how can anything exist that is not God? In fact, nothing exists which is not God. Everything in existence has its "being" in God. Everything is God-stuff. We have already addressed this.

The truth is not dependent on your approval, and one thing that is absolutely true is that reality (all of it) contains everything that exists. This includes evil and darkness.

Everything that exists has a purpose. Nothing is excluded from this. Even if you say that something is an illusion, it has a reason for existing *as an illusion*. All things are supported by God the Creator, or they would not exist.

We explained in the chapters on the ego that evil, darkness, fear, chaos, unconsciousness, etc. are all part of what the ego creates in order to force the soul to balance it with light. We explained that evil (darkness) is the fertilizer that strengthens and grows both the soul and the ego. We also explained that you grow spiritually by overcoming the darkness that you have created.

FIRST THINGS FIRST

First the ego creates darkness, and then the soul balances it with light. First we create chaos, and then we bring order to it. First we make mistakes, and then we learn from them. First we incur karma, and then we balance it.

There is no evil where we come from. One of the biggest reasons we are here is to experience evil, as it is the greatest tool for our growth.

Please do not misunderstand. This does *not* mean that we should seek to be evil or that we should try to be evil. There is no need to try, because *we already are*. The ego already provides all of the darkness that is needed. That is what it does. If you look around at the world and at yourself, you will see that evil comes from one place only: the human mind. And, as you know, we have plenty of evil here.

The darkness is already here. Overcoming it is our lofty task. In creating and overcoming our own darkness, we grow, and so does the Whole (God).

DO WE HAVE FREE WILL?

"Free will" allows you to choose between the polarities of light and dark. "Freedom of choice" allows you to choose between various neutral options like chicken or steak, Burger King or McDonalds.

The polarities are what we are speaking about here. These are the *left hand* of God, Archangel Lucifer, the anchor of the dark. And the *right hand* of God, Archangel Michael, the anchor of the light. Out of darkness comes light, and out of matter (matter is darkness) comes spirit.

Freewill, incarnation, reincarnation, and karma govern your process of ascension or return. They govern your growth. However, free will is a tricky subject because you don't have the freedom that you think you do.

The ego ascends through darkness and will choose darkness every time. The soul ascends through light and will choose light every time. This is what they must do, what they are designed and commanded to do. However, where are "you" in all of this?

Your body and brain are caught in the middle of this tug of war, believing that you have the freedom to choose whatever you want; believing that you have free will. But, as we said previously, *you are not you!* You think that you are the body and the mind, but this is the false self – an illusion. This false thinking must be reconciled if you are to know who you are and live from the heart center. To live from the heart center is to be led by the Spirit, to be led by your Divine Self.

You have freedom of choice, but do you have free will? It has certainly been made to appear like you have free will. It must appear that way in order to allow the game of God to play out unnoticed by most. Most think they have all of the freedom in the world, and yet they are unaware of the ego making choices for them. They believe those choices and thoughts are their own. They believe they are coming from "them." Observe your mind for yourself and see what you find.

Try to grasp that one cannot *think* God. God is neither rational nor reasonable to the ego/mind. God cannot be *sensed* through the five senses, but only *felt* through the heart center. If you think it, or if it comes through the mind, then it comes from the ego. Its purposes conflict with the heart center, and it is no longer love based.

We will touch on the subject of free will again in the discussion about karma.

THE BALANCE BETWEEN LIGHT AND DARK

Creation is always in balance. Creation must be in balance. Balance is a fundamental principle of this universe. Balance can be seen everywhere. It is a fact. Wherever balance is temporarily lost, it is immediately sought again. We could give example after example from daily life and the physics of nature, but as for you, spiritually speaking, you must always be in balance between light and dark.

The Creator is grown through the combination of increasing darkness and balancing with an equal amount of light. Remember, he is all things. Whether you are increasing darkness or light, either one, you are increasing him. Darkness is increased in order to increase the light, and darkness isn't bad, it is the Creator too. Look at darkness as matter. Most people want to run from the darkness, but you need to realize that you are *both*. You are the darkness too.

MORE LIGHT MEANS MORE DARKNESS ALSO

Since darkness is increased first and then light is sent to balance, the greater the light you are, the greater the darkness you are also. There is no greatly evolved light being on this planet that is not equal in darkness. Darkness and light must always be in balance. The greater the light, the greater the darkness.

You, humanity, are the evil. Surely you can see this in the world around you and in yourself. However, you are *also* the great lights. You can also see this in yourself and in the world. And what about the body? The body is a tool for both light and dark to play out the game of God. The body is the "soil" in which you grow.

So please understand that, in this world, darkness is increased *through you*, and then light is sent to balance *through you*. Light comes from one source, above the firmament in the Celestial realm. Darkness is generated here in this physical realm only.

THERE IS NO EVIL WHERE WE COME FROM

All of you came here to experience evil. Where we come from there is no evil. Not only is there no evil to stimulate growth, but there is also no material flesh body to place the spirit within. The seed that you are must be placed into soil to grow and then be fertilized to stimulate the growth. Darkness is that fertilizer.

Again, you all came here to experience evil, because where we come from there is none. And it doesn't matter whether you think you are from the 5th, the 6th, the 7th dimension, or above that. Even if you think "I am a Creator God," it makes no difference because you came here to experience the same evil as everyone else.

LIGHT FROM DARKNESS IS HOW THE CREATOR GROWS

You came to experience the darkness because it is how the Creator grows himself by growing you. Darkness is created (generated) by the ego. The ego is a soul too, your soul mate. Light is then sent by the Angel to match. Each time that happens you have become larger, spiritually speaking.

As you grow through each incarnation, you increase darkness and light is sent to match. Every time this happens you have become bigger. When the body fills, what you have grown is taken and put into the Astral, on your "account" you might say, which is you.

YOU ARE NOT THE BODY

Understand that you have several bodies. You have an Earthly 3D body (flesh body), you have your ego body (electromagnetic body), and you have the Astral body, which is your soul's body. You have all of these, but what you are building is the Light Body. And you started building this with your first incarnation. The Light Body is what you will return in.

You are not the flesh body. The physical 3D Earthly flesh body will not go to the Celestial realm. It does not matter how you change it. There are some who even believe that the DNA will be modified to allow this flesh body to travel to the Celestial. This is not true. Many want to believe that because they are hoping to leave here without experiencing death. Some believe this, but it is not true. Death of the physical body is inevitable. The physical body was made for the physical realm, and that is where it will stay. It was assembled from dust, and to dust will it return. But it is *not* who or what you are.

To become what you really are, a great Angel, you must overcome *through* the flesh. And what is it that you must overcome? Darkness. Every time you overcome darkness by having light sent from your Angel to balance that darkness, you get larger.

By overcoming you become.

You are the God of YOU. You are in charge of your own growth, and in overcoming, you grow yourself. You create yourself. You awaken yourself. As you do this for yourself, you do it for God too.

Darkness is the catalyst which allows the growth to happen. You cannot bring just light into the body. It doesn't work. You will be out of balance. Your contribution to the Creator and yourself will cease until you come back into balance.

DON'T MESS WITH A PERFECT SYSTEM

Let me elaborate further on how balance works so it isn't misunderstood. The ego is the catalyst. It stimulates the growth. It incurs the darkness gradually, trespass by trespass. It does not bring great amounts of darkness into the body. Why? *Because the flesh body suffers the effect.* Darkness is brought into the vessel gradually, and light is sent to balance gradually. The vessel is like a glass that is filled slowly with dark and then light throughout the entire lifetime, always maintaining balance.

To those who say, "I bring light into my body through meditation" or "I am calling in the light to fill my being," let me say this: You know not what you do! In overloading yourself to any one side, light or dark, you are setting yourself up for an equal amount of the opposite polarity to be immediately brought into the body. Know that if you fill yourself with light, causing yourself to be out of balance to the light side, you will be subject to an equal or greater amount of darkness. You will most likely experience what many call "the dark night of the soul."

The ego is a master of bringing in darkness in amounts that the body can handle and transmute. The soul is a master of bringing light to that darkness. It is the creature, you, that causes your own difficulties. God's system is perfect. Understand it, but don't mess with it!

Balance is a fundamental property of creation. Light and dark must always be in balance. The greater the light, the greater the darkness.

WHY DO WE INCARNATE?

You incarnate the first time *to incur karma*. You reincarnate again *to clear or balance karma*. Eventually, through incarnation, you balance all karma and are finished in the 3D world, yet you may choose to come back to help others and to continue growing yourself. This places you in a different relationship to karma, which we will discuss later, but you are always subject to the karmic system as long as you are in the physical world. This book lays out step by step how that system, God's system, works. However, incurring and clearing karma are not the only reasons we incarnate.

TO MODIFY GENETICS

We also incarnate to modify the genetics of the body that we are incarnating into. Very slowly, generation by generation, life forms are modified this way. What has the human form been modified to do? To carry more light! Light is awareness or Presence.

The Christ was the crowning achievement of this in this world. The genetics of the Hebrews were modified again and again over many generations in order to create the Christ. This was their purpose and what they achieved.

The Christ, "Elect One," or "Mashiac," was he who could carry all of the light (spirit) of the world in him, and return it to the Father in the Celestial realm. This was Michael who became Christ, Lord of the Universe. All spiritual material (souls) has been fragmented from him in the last 2,000 or so years. 1 Corinthians 12:11 – "That one and same Spirit (Christ) dividing to every man, individually, as he will."

And just to clear up another one of the false rumors that has been created, we must say this: No one modifies your genetics except you. Not the Annunaki, not Planet X, nor aliens from outer space. You do it to you, by bringing light to darkness, by growing.

TO EXPERIENCE EVIL

We explained this one in the previous chapter. You came here to experience evil and darkness. There is no evil and no darkness where we come from. Evil is the catalyst or fertilizer that stimulates the growth of light that we came here to accomplish.

TO PROVIDE "FOOD"

The byproducts of incarnation are a kind of energy or light or "food" that is provided from both your ego and your soul, and through them to both the planetary consciousness (Lucifer) and your Angel. From there, all of creation, the rest of the way up, is fed. You grow and feed the rest of yourself and the entire body of God, the All in All, from here. All of this is done through the mixture of dark and light which is brought into your body through incarnation.

TO CREATE YOURSELF ABOVE

What is your reason for being here? *To create yourself above through the flesh below.* What is your purpose? It is to carry out God's plan, which is to merge all things in Heaven (spirit) with all things on Earth (matter). Your purpose is to bring all of the light (spirit) of your higher self, your Divine Self, your Angel, your Elohim, or your God (whatever you want to call it) into form. When you have done this you are finished, you are done incarnating.

You incarnate through the cycles, with your purpose being to merge Heaven and Earth in your flesh. You bring light to darkness, spirit to matter. Spirit grows out of matter, and matter is transformed into spirit.

TO BUILD THE LIGHT BODY

Through incarnation you are building something. What you are building is the Light Body. With each incarnation you are bringing light to darkness, and you are growing. What you grow is placed in the Astral. When you reincarnate, the "you" from the Astral is placed into your flesh body, which is made out of what? You.

You incarnate within genetic lines. It is your line. You built it. You created it. You increase your light through darkness with every incarnation, with every single one. You create the flesh body that will be based on the amount of light that you have brought to the darkness placed in the Astral.

Again, your purpose is to bring in all of you above, and when it is in, you are done. You have finished the creation of the Light Body or 5D body or Celestial body. You are a little seed that grows in the soil (flesh body). With each incarnation the seed gets bigger and bigger and bigger, but you cannot return or ascend without the Light Body. It is the body that you have been building through all of your incarnations. The physical body will remain in the physical. It isn't going anywhere. You can believe whatever you want. You can believe that it is becoming crystalline or that the DNA is being activated (many teach these things), but it is a physical body and it will stay physical.

You have an Astral body which can go to the Astral. This is the soul's body that you already have. But the 5D Celestial body is the one that you have been building. That is what all of us have incarnated over and over to accomplish. We have incarnated to grow spiritually through the flesh body, bringing light to darkness, until we have reached a point where our light (vibration) is equal to the Celestial realm.

WE RETURN IN THE LIGHT BODY

When we have finished incarnating, and return to the Celestial realm from which we came, we will do it in the Light Body.

Please do not worry or stress over this. Both ego and soul are contained within the Light Body. The two shall be made one, so that even though you will lose your 3D physical body that you have become so attached to, you will not lose any of the memories of anything that happened in that lifetime. You will still be you, just in an eternal form! In fact, finally, you will be privy to all of your incarnations. You will not lose one memory from all of your time incarnate!

Rest assured, the 3D body will no longer be necessary. You will continue!

WHAT IS A WALK-IN?

Simply put, a "walk-in" is a soul transference or exchange. One soul leaves the body and another, higher version from the same Angel, comes in and takes its place. The soul that left could technically be referred to as a "walk-out." The walk-in is actually the new soul which takes its place. As opposed to being "born in" and growing up with the body, the new soul has "walked in" directly, bypassing the long maturing process.

Often, but not always, walk-ins occur following traumatic life experiences such as illnesses, accidents, loss of loved ones, or exposure to prolonged darkness without balancing by light.

The possibility of a soul exchange may seem strange and disturbing to some, especially the first time they hear of it. But remember, you are not the body. You are that which inhabits the body. The body is just "clothes for God." It is a vehicle that you use to live out your purpose here.

Another concern may be that we are talking about some sort of possession. Well, you *do* possess your body. This is a fact. However, a walk-in is nothing like inviting another entity into your body (which should not be done, generally speaking). We are *not* talking about demon possession here. In fact, as we have said, the "demon" is your ego. In a walk-out/walk-in scenario it is actually the soul that is exchanged, *not* the ego.

The ego remains with the body, and since the ego records and maintains the memories, they remain with the body as well. So a walk-in can occur without the conscious awareness of the person (human), since they may still feel like the same "self." Others, however, will more easily notice any changes in personality or habits after a walk-in.

A walk-in is like being connected to a stronger power source. After an adjustment period, the body typically becomes healthier, and there is an increase in awareness. Over time the person will tend to become more interested in spiritual matters and the truths of existence, as they become aware in ways that they were not previously.

Walk-ins have been on the rise since about the 1950's and there are several reasons why they occur, but the subject is too large to fully explain here. We dedicated five two-hour radio shows to this subject, which can be found on YouTube and the BlogTalkRadio archives. We are also writing another book specifically about walk-ins.

NUMEROLOGY AND BIRTH NUMBERS

The Creator's system for incarnation is not random. Everything functions in a precise order to bring about a precise outcome. One grows spiritually through incarnation in a physical body, which we have addressed briefly in the previous chapters.

The seed or soul, a small fragment of consciousness, is placed within the soil to grow. In this case, the soil is your body. Through incarnation, one grows in light. The more you incarnate, the bigger and greater you become, spiritually speaking. There is an exact system whereby each seed incarnates and reincarnates to grow itself. Each seed is subject to the "9 cycle" of incarnations. You begin as a "1" and finish as a "9." The 1 level is about "beginning" or "self," whereby you begin to incur karma. The 9 level is about completion, in which you have cleared or balanced all incurred karma. All begin as a 1 and end as a 9. There is no jumping around in the 1-9 scale, it is a linear progression up the scale.

In addition to the 1-9 incarnations there are what we call Master numbers or Master vibrations, which are 11, 22, 33 and sometimes 44. These are souls who have completed the mandatory incarnation cycles, balanced all karma, and have chosen to return to assist humanity and to continue their own growth. We will explain more about Master vibrations later in the book.

Through the incarnation cycles you grow in light and become larger, spiritually speaking. Thus said, it is safe to say that you have become more spiritually aware with each incarnation. It is a natural progression up the spiritual ladder to your return, so to speak.

FIND YOUR OWN NUMBER

You can find your own personal number (vibration or life path) by adding together all of the numbers of your birth date. This will allow you to see where you are on the incarnation wheel or cycle.

Two examples:
June 27, 1970 => 0+6+2+7+1+9+7+0 = 32 = 3+2 = 5
December 16, 1994 => 1+2+1+6+1+9+9+4 = 33 (Master)

You continue to add the single digits together until you get one final single digit. If at any point you arrive at a Master number (11, 22, 33 and sometimes 44) you *stop* and do not reduce any further.

The basic numbers are 1 through 9. 1 is the beginning, or self, and 9 is completion. Through the system you start as a 1, which is the only single digit number where you come in with no karma. You begin to create your karma for all of your incarnations. You begin it as a 1.

Karma is incurred in one lifetime and worked off in the next lifetime. So you start from a 1, which is incurring karma, and then in the 2 lifetime you begin to clear the karma. You are also incurring karma for the next lifetime while you are working off karma from the previous lifetime.

So you go up the scale from 1 to 9, life by life, with 9 being completion. But you may do each lifetime several times. It may take you three or four lifetimes to complete the 2 incarnation. You complete the lifetime by balancing most all of the darkness or karma incurred in the 2 lifetime. Once you do, you will advance to the 3 lifetime, which is communication. Then 4, which is work. Five is change. Six is family. Seven is spirituality. Eight is wealth and power. And nine is completion.

Nine is the toughest lifetime because it is the *completion* lifetime. It is the toughest because you are both incurring karma in that lifetime and also balancing it in the same lifetime. At the completion of the 9 lifetime you must be karma free in order to be finished.

The 9 lifetime also prepares you for the Master incarnations, if you decide to make that choice. Why? Because, in the later stages of the 9 incarnation, you will be subject to instant karma, and this is the same program that all Masters are on (in regard to karma).

A WALK-IN CHANGES THE NUMEROLOGY

We must mention walk-ins again briefly here because it can change things quite dramatically when it comes to the birth number/path. All walk-in souls are at least an 11 or higher, regardless of the birth number of their body, ego, and previous soul.

Again, this subject is vast and has been addressed by many hours of online teaching. It is beyond the scope of this book and yet must be at least somewhat understood in order for the rest of the discussion to make sense.

Suffice it to say that if you are a walk-in (and you may be one without consciously knowing it yet) then your birth number will not hold the weight that it does in the cases where the original soul remains with the body. When a walk-in occurs it will always be a more advanced soul with the minimum level being 11. If you are understanding this book or it quickly resonates with you, and you are one of the basic single digit numbers, then chances are that you are a walk-in. Most lower numbers will have serious difficulty with the simplicity of this work.

We will further explain the difference between the single digits and the Master numbers as part of the discussion later in the book. For now we will just say that the way they fit into the karma system is one of the main differences between them.

ASCENSION AND KARMA ARE CONSIDERED EASTERN AND NEW AGE BUT YOU REFERENCE THE BIBLE?

Yes. The Bible is the greatest spiritual book ever written, but only if you can understand the spiritual wisdom contained within it. It is not a religious book nor is it a book about religion. Nor did Christ come to start a religion. When you understand the metaphors, which are consistent throughout the Bible, and you understand (or better yet, remember for yourself) the spiritual history of this world which the Bible documents, then and only then will the Bible make sense, spiritually speaking, without religion being involved.

By the way, we do not only reference the Bible, but also the Gnostic Gospels and the Dead Sea Scrolls and the Nag Hammadi, and the Urantia Book. Allfaaraa's teachings can be verified in all of these esoteric works.

You will find that the Creator's truth does not fall into any one man-made category. It is not just Eastern or Western. Not just New Age or Christian. It is not even isolated to this one universe.

Fragments of the truth can be found everywhere, yet the whole truth reunites these fragments.

WHAT IS KARMA?

Karma is the law of cause and effect, right? No! Karma is the Divine system, or program, which governs the entire 3D (physical) creation and controls and balances the growth of spirit in this universe. Karma is the system which allows the Creator (or Whole) to grow, through growing you, the parts. As the parts grow, through the incurring and clearing of karma, the Creator grows also.

How it works is so simple it's astounding. Darkness and light must always remain in balance. Remember, the Creator is all things. He declares in Isaiah 45:7 – "I am the light and I am the dark, I make peace and I create evil." He is all things, so no matter what is created, good or bad, black or white, he is grown. He always gains, no matter what happens.

The ego is active, and the soul is passive. The ego drives and forces the growth of the soul through the choices that it makes and the actions that it takes.

The Creator's system for growth contains three components that all go together: **incarnation, free will, and karma.**

You incarnate to grow karma, and you reincarnate to clear karma. Why is that? Because, as a 1-9 soul, karma is being incurred in this lifetime that you will work off in the next lifetime. Working off karma grows both you and the Creator.

This system (past-life karma) is not applied to Master

vibrations (11, 22, 33 and walk-ins). But it does apply to all those incarnate between the numbers (life paths) of 1 through 9. The karma that you have incurred in the last lifetime is worked off in the current lifetime. However, walk-ins are on the same program as all Master vibrations. Once the karma from the previous soul is cleared, you, the walk-in, are subject to the same rules as any other Master vibration, which is instant karma, which we will address later.

THE MOST VEILED LIFETIME

If any of you are familiar with hypnotic regression, most of the lifetimes that appear are many lifetimes into the past. You usually are not allowed in any way, shape, or form to see or have access to, your last incarnation. One of the reasons for this is that you are veiled to your most recent karma incurred and how it was incurred. This is because of the way the ego works. It is very smart and very tricky. If it knows its direct past karma, it will attempt to figure a way around it, thus stunting your growth and the growth of God. The heaviest veil that each and every one of us has is on the last lifetime. The most recent lifetime is the least likely to show up in regression.

So, back to the question. What is karma? Karma is the Divine system ordained, or put into effect, that insures the growth of spirit, the growth of God. It ensures that each individual soul, through their karma incurred and then cleared, will grow spiritually. Karma ensures that this is your greatest lifetime. You have never been more, spiritually speaking, than you are right now in this lifetime.

WHAT KARMA IS NOT

When asked what karma is, most will say, *"you reap what you sow."* And yet, this is false.

The term "you reap what you sow" comes from Paul and directly out of the New Testament of the Scriptures. It has nothing to do with karma at all. "Sow" means to either scatter, plant, or grow. "Reap" means to harvest. It is referring directly to you the seed or soul. What you grow, you get. If you grow gold, you get gold (metaphorically speaking). If you grow dirt, you get dirt. If you grow wheat, you get wheat. What is grown in the soil (your body) is what comes back. That is exactly what that means. It has nothing whatsoever to do with karma.

"You reap what you sow" has nothing to do with karma, and yet that is the concept that most people attach to the system, and that everyone else has adopted. You reap what you sow...false! That means "you get what you grow." Which is true, but it has nothing to do with karma.

The next most common misunderstanding is *"the law of cause and effect."* False! That is another fallacy. You could call it New Age fiction. Karma is not *a law*. The law, even to the Hebrews, was not a law. So karma is not a law, it is a Divine program or system placed into effect (ordained) by the Creator to govern all of creation. And to govern it how? To keep it (the creation) in balance. The Creator, and thereby the entire creation, grows through balance. It can also be said that it actually frees up God. Yet God is already free because he is passive. He does not do the work. But karma is a Divine program that allows, governs, and balances creation. It governs the rate of ascension (growth) of every single seed/soul on the planet under the firmament. And no Lord, Archangel, or Christ is in charge of administering it.

Karma is fully self-supervised. There is no God of karma.

So, in summary, karma is *not* about reaping what you sow, and it is *not* the law of cause and effect. As we move ahead we will explain exactly what it is in detail, and how it works.

THE TWO TYPES OF KARMA

Let us state what karma is just one more time before we continue. Karma is *the Divine system controlling the growth of spirit (God) in this world,* which is below the firmament. It ensures that, sooner or later, most all will become, and most all will return or ascend.

It does not make any difference whether you believe in God, don't believe in God, are spiritual or not spiritual. All serve. All participate. Karma ensures that every seed/soul will grow spiritually by overcoming darkness and balancing it with light. And every time that happens you get larger (spiritually) and so does the Creator.

There are two types of karma. Let us call them "normal karma," which is what you incur in your incarnations 1 through 9 up through the ladder. And there is "instant karma," which all Master vibrations have. All incarnate are subject to karma of one kind or another. As a Master vibration you have no past karma carried forth from a previous lifetime. You cannot have existing karma and directly serve the Creator. That is why you are subject to instant karma.

All who are incarnate incur karma. However, Master vibrations, which are 11, 22 and 33 on the numerological scale, are direct servants of the Creator. They must be karma free (balanced) at all times. They, alone, are subject to instant karma.

UNDERSTANDING KARMA IS IMPORTANT

Even though some are karma free, everyone still needs to understand karma because karma is an important key in understanding the game of God. It is the system that controls and affects everything in this universe.

As a soul incarnate, and especially as a Master vibration, you need to know every aspect of God's plan, God's rules, and God's system. The more you know of the Creator the closer you come to him. As the Creator has spoken, "Come near to me, and I will come near to you." The closer your purpose aligns to his purpose, the more he manifests his/her providence (love, protection, forgiveness) over you.

Most of those that study with me are Master teachers and yet, like most all of humanity, they still look to others for their understandings; books, websites, teachers, healers, astrologers, counselors. Mankind's spiritual knowledge is an assembly of cut and pasted works from other people. I am going to teach you directly from God so you will know more than anybody else. We begin in this first book with the system that all are under when they begin to incarnate in this world.

NO ONE IS EXEMPT FROM KARMA

Everybody is under a certain type of karma, either normal karma, if incarnate between 1 and 9, or instant karma, if incarnate as an 11, 22, 33 or walk-in. There is no such thing as "no karma," or somehow being exempt from karma. You can be "karma free," but that does not mean that you are not still subject to the karmic system itself. You may be balanced and free at the moment, but you are not outside of, or above, the system of karma. All here in this world are subject to karma. The 11's, 22's and 33's (Master vibrations) are all subject to instant karma, and that serves to maintain balance and keep them clear to perform the Creator's work, not their own.

NORMAL KARMA

Normal karma is incurred a lifetime behind. It is incurred in this lifetime and balanced in the next, or subsequent, lifetimes. This applies to all those in the 1-9 cycle on the numerology scale, which is still a majority of the people on the planet. You incur karma in this life and balance it in the next. This makes the final lifetime, the 9, the most difficult, because not only are you incurring karma from the current lifetime which must be balanced, but you are also balancing karma from the previous lifetime. At the end of a completed 9 incarnation all karma must be balanced, both from the current lifetime and the previous lifetime, in order to ascend or return.

INSTANT KARMA

Instead of clearing karma incurred in the past lifetime that you are working off in this current lifetime, karma earned in this lifetime can be cleared within minutes or within days. That is what we refer to as instant karma. It doesn't really go any longer than that. In other words, for you to serve the Creator as a Master vibration, you cannot have existing karma.

Why is that?

WHY CAN'T YOU DIRECTLY SERVE THE CREATOR WITH EXISTING KARMA?

The Creator has rules and laws in place. Everything counters the other to maintain balance between the polarities, light and dark. It is such a perfect system when you understand it and know it as the Angels do. You just have to say, "Wow, this Creator must really be God or something!"

You can't have karma as a direct servant because it is contradictory to God's program and plan for you. The soul's first purpose, when incarnate in a flesh body, is to incur and clear karma. Understand that, for a 1-9 soul on normal karma, you are incurring karma in the current lifetime to clear in the next, while also clearing the karma that you incurred from the previous lifetime. What a game we are caught up in!

The soul's first purpose is to clear karma, but you could also say that the soul's purpose is to grow God. That is the ultimate purpose. But in working off karma you are growing God (through growing yourself). This is the end result. That is how it works. But the soul's first purpose is to work off and remove karma. In so doing it grows itself.

However, when you are a direct servant of the Creator, as a God, an Angel, an Archangel or soul incarnate (a Master vibration 11, 22, 33), if you had existing karma, your first service would be to *yourself* and not to the Creator.

So, in serving yourself by incarnating to clear previous karma, you could not be directly serving the Creator because your purpose would conflict with his purpose, which is serving humanity. In other words, when you reincarnate to clear past karma, your first purpose is to clear that karma. Your second is to serve, to grow the Creator through growing yourself. However, in fulfilling your first purpose you are fulfilling the second automatically.

This is why you cannot have karma, because, as a direct servant of the Creator, it is whatever he decides. You'll serve darkness. You'll serve light. You'll do any number of things. And it may be in direct conflict with the soul's first purpose. This is why Masters who serve the Creator, and who serve humanity, cannot have any karma. They must constantly be in balance.

Thus said, you cannot serve humanity with karma on your books. Even a Master, when he/she has karma, is taken out of the game and placed "on the bench." You are no longer serving in any capacity while you have karma, even though you may be a world karma server. Until the darkness is balanced, you are a worthless servant. That is why instant karma is, well, instant.

HOW DOES KARMA WORK?

Here is how karma works for those incarnate in the numbers between 1 and 9, which is about 65% of humanity.

Keep in mind, and we haven't explained this yet, but there is no good karma and there is no bad karma. There is karma, period. Karma is earned, incurred, or acquired (whatever word you want to use) when you commit a trespass against another soul incarnate; when you trespass against another human. A "cause" is incurred when you take advantage of, cheat, lie to, harm, or otherwise try to force someone to do something, or act according to *your* will.

Simply stated, a trespass is something that is not "correct action." It is any way that you enforce your will or attempt to take advantage of someone else. It doesn't matter if it is for gain or not, which it normally would be or you wouldn't do it.

A trespass is the "cause," and it will result in an "effect," which is the karma and the necessary balancing of it. Darkness is cause and light is effect.

It could be just enforcing your will or ideas. Or it could be stealing, revenge, etc. Even lying to your children to get them to go to bed is a trespass. For example, you might say, "If you don't go to bed now, the boogie man is coming to get you," or something like that. You have just committed a trespass.

Any act or thought intended to cause anything untrue, or to manipulate or control another person's free will or freedom of choice, is a trespass. – To manipulate, to sway, to enforce one's will, or to induce an outcome.

This is what karma is. And when it happens karma is applied to you. Or you could say that darkness is increased to you. Karma really is just darkness applied to your account. This is how the system works.

Here is a question that came up which helps to clarify what is meant.

"I take care of my mother-in-law who has Alzheimer's and sometimes I try to get her to do things and there is no longer a functioning mind up there."

No, that does not count. You would not incur karma having to get somebody in that position to do something that they don't want to do. Now, if they have Alzheimer's and you are stealing money out of their bank account because they won't remember it, well then in that case, you will be getting some heavy karma. But if you are just trying to get them to go to sleep or eat, or something else for *their* benefit, then there is no trespass.

IT HAPPENS AUTOMATICALLY

How does one increase darkness? By incurring karma for yourself. And it's automatic. This is critical and so very simple! It is that easy. You don't have to go out and intentionally increase darkness to bring more light. *It is automatic.* Your choices control the karma received. This is why free will is necessary so you can acquire karma at your own pace. Actually we are getting ahead of the questions here as to how we control karma.

Your choices control the level of karma that you acquire in order to grow. Incurred karma, and the balancing of that karma, is necessary to return or ascend. Another way to look at it is this: Karma is the Divine tool which you administer to control your ascension.

DIFFERENT LEVELS OF TRESPASS

There are different levels of trespasses. There are slight trespasses, for instance, but they are still trespasses. They will incur, let us say, one measure of karma. There are also trespasses that incur three measures of karma. There are trespasses that incur five measures of karma. Karma is not balanced in an "eye for an eye" fashion or in equal measures. Although it was at times, especially to the Angels of Israel, the 144,000 now incarnate again.

Understand that light is not sent to balance darkness measure for measure, not all at once anyway. If you were an abuser in one lifetime, that doesn't necessarily mean you will be abused in this lifetime, although many people believe that is the case. But each trespass carries its own measure of darkness.

You have to remember that you are incarnate for, God willing, an entire lifetime. Not just 30 years and not just 50 years. Also understand this: Most of your karma is incurred after the age of 18. It does not start when you are 12, 13, or 14. You are not incurring karma when you are a child. Thus said, you are growing neither light nor darkness.

Starting around the age of 18 is when karma starts to be incurred. This starts to happen when the soul is mature, around the same age souls begin to grow and transfer light. They start to awaken at about the 18 year level, and they incur most of the karma in their lifetime between about 18 and 35 years old. Then you spend the rest of your life, from 35 on, working the darn stuff off. The karma that you are incurring is going to be applied to the next lifetime. So you are incurring for the next lifetime while working off, or clearing, from the previous lifetime.

We are all busy, busy, busy doing the Creator's work, yet most all of us haven't a clue. We have no idea why we are here and what our purpose is. And we wander aimlessly through each incarnation.

Karma ensures that, no matter what, most all who are incarnate will grow; even if they have no clue as to why they are here and what they need to do!

WHAT IS THE PURPOSE OF KARMA?

The purpose of karma, its ultimate purpose, is to grow God through growing "you," the aspect of God. It is the system that ensures that, no matter what happens, *God wins.*

This is what is so great about the game. If you are good, what happens to God? He grows. If you are bad, what happens? He still grows. *You still pay the penalty,* but no matter what happens, the Creator wins. He wins by growing and becoming larger and more aware, *through you.*

It is an automatic system. The Creator has nothing to do with it, except that he implemented it. So no matter what, like death and taxes, karma guarantees that the Creator (and you) will grow spiritually. Is that a perfect system or what?

As an example, imagine if you throw some seeds out there to plant corn, and then someone comes along and waters them and fertilizes them. You, as God, do not have to do anything. But no matter what happens they keep growing. Sometimes a little fertilizer is necessary. That fertilizer is darkness.

Nothing can interfere with the system. You dictate the amount of growth by the amount of darkness that you bring upon yourself. Remember, darkness brought on by the ego is the catalyst, and you create that darkness. The more darkness you create, the more light that must be sent to balance it. So, the greater the trespass, the greater the light required to balance the trespass.

Understand that God's system for this 3D world is based on cause and effect. *What is caused in the flesh below has its effect in the Spirit above.* God increases himself through your flesh. That is how it works. But what he is increasing is "you" since you are in him.

By increasing the parts (each of us) he increases the Whole (all of him). *It's that simple.*

IS THERE GOOD KARMA AND BAD KARMA?

No, there is no good karma, and there is no bad karma. There is just karma, period.

When people say, "If I do this good act, I will get good karma," that is wrong. There is no good karma. If you have karma, it is not a good thing, because that means you have darkness on your books, and you are subject to overcoming that darkness. Your cause is now subject to effect. You have bad "juju" on your chop board, and that juju is going to be cleaned. The cleaning of that bad juju is usually painful in some way, and that is why we often refer to karma as "bad."

There is no bad karma or good karma. All karma is "bad" in that it is darkness on your books. When you hear "good karma," stop and correct the person.

Karma is simply darkness applied to your account. That darkness then requires balancing with light. You overcome the darkness by balancing it with light, and each time this happens you grow, and the Creator also grows, spiritually speaking.

The ego grows through darkness, and the soul through light. The ego is the catalyst, as it is active. The soul is passive.

Even though all karma is perceived as "bad," the Creator and the Angels and Archangels would inform you that, without karma, there would be no growth of light. Therefore, is it ultimately "bad"? Or is it part of a complete system which, on the whole, is "good"?

It may seem confusing that in one sentence we say that there is no such thing as good and bad karma, and then in the next sentence we say all karma is bad. However, the point is that it is *bad* from one perspective (yours, because of the pain of balancing it out again), but it is *good* from another higher perspective (God's), because of the growth it brings to your soul and ego, and therefore also the Whole.

"So what we were calling good karma incorrectly is the law of attraction working, right? Good energy attracts good energy?"

No, there is no law of attraction that has anything to do with karma. There is no law of attraction affecting karma. Put that out of your mind. Karma is not a law. It has nothing to do with the law. It is a system, a Divine system. Karma is Divine. Bless it. Every time you get karma, every time you do something bad, thank God because out of it you are becoming. This is critical. Out of chaos comes order. You are that chaos! Yet through the karmic system you will become order.

Karma is actually a blessing. When you have karma, you are blessed, because you are being balanced. You are being increased, this is how it works. Whether you label it good or bad will depend on your perspective, but either way it is just karma, period.

Understand this: no karma, no growth.

WHO HAS KARMA?

Every single person/human/soul in this 3D physical realm is subject to the system of karma.

All of those who are incarnating in the cycles 1 through 9 have existing karma, but things are a little different for the 1's and the 9's compared to the other basic numbers.

As I told you before, when you begin the incarnation cycle you come in as a 1. At that point you are a new fragment (seed/soul), and you come in without any karma. So the entire 1 incarnation is based on the self. It is all about you, and this is how you begin your incarnations. You do not care much for understanding spiritual things, and you trespass, and you trespass, and you trespass! You are like a seed that is preparing its own soil. The 1 incarnation is where you incur the karma to start you down the path. The beginning incarnation does not allow you to work off or clear karma because you don't have any karma. In the 1 incarnation you earn/incur karma to start yourself down the path.

The 9 incarnation is about completion, and is actually the hardest incarnation, because it's the one that takes the most lifetimes to finish. Why? Because not only you working off karma from your lifetimes as an 8 (because karma is posted a lifetime behind), but you are actually incurring karma as a 9 also, aren't you? You are both increasing and decreasing karma in the same incarnation, but you are decreasing karma from two lifetimes at once, the previous one and the current one.

The 9 is the toughest incarnation and usually takes multiple attempts to complete. But to do it in one is almost impossible because, again, you are clearing karma from the past life, and you are incurring karma in the present life, and you have to clear or balance it all. In order to complete the incarnation cycles on this planet, one must remove and balance all existing karma. A 9 soul has done this through all of the cycles and all previous incarnations. So obviously it is much larger, spiritually speaking, than an 8 soul or a 7 soul.

ALL INCARNATIONS ARE SUBJECT TO KARMA

The 1 incarnation and the 9 incarnation are different than all of the others, but all incarnations are subject to karma. When karma is balanced as a 9 incarnation, and after those lifetimes have been completed, you will be given the option to continue here in 3D as a Master vibration. You already are karma free. You have achieved ascension because your vibration matches the next realm after completion of the 9 cycle. Also, you have earned the necessary level of Spirit to continue, if you chose to continue in form, and take the next step. You begin as an 11 which is the lowest Master vibration. You do not have any karma. You enter clear and balanced from the 1–9 cycle.

Remember, you cannot have existing karma and serve the Creator as a Master vibration because the purposes conflict. The soul's first purpose is what? The first purpose would be to take care of your karma, to clear it. In clearing karma you grow God and yourself, so they are basically the same. When karma exists on your account, so to speak, the soul's first purpose is to do what it takes to clear or balance its karma. So, again, that is a direct conflict with the Creator's purpose for you as a Master, which is to serve him as he decides. The first purpose (for a Master) has to be serving the Creator, not clearing your karma. So you must always be in balance and have no karma. This is why all Masters are subject to instant karma. In order to maintain balance, the trespass must be immediately resolved.

Also, when you commit a trespass, since you are a Master incarnate, you are more aware of the potential results. And as a Master you begin to understand "egoically," because you learn, as the ego, that when you do things, there are consequences. If I am bad, bad things happen to me. You understand that it is not random. You understand that you are the cause, and you are the effect as well.

Remember, the ego creates the karma that the soul balances. So karma is darkness. The soul balances the darkness by bringing light to the darkness that the ego creates. Every single seed incarnate, every single body that is human, is subject to and has karma, unless you are a Master where you are subject to instant karma. And again, that can be balanced almost instantaneously or, at the most, within a couple of days. But it isn't going to go a week, because while you have incurred that darkness, you are taken out of service to the Creator. You are no longer serving while you are out of balance, so that is why it is instant. It happens immediately in order to keep you serving him. We have covered this, yet I will continue to repeat some things to impress them upon your egos.

Instant karma can work in weird ways. It does not have to be as violent and obvious as being run over by a car. Because again, those Master vibrations that are subject to instant karma are highly evolved spiritual beings, and they have incarnated enough that their egos understand what is right and what is wrong.

What I am saying is that your ego has an idea of what correct action is, and you also have an awareness of it when you do bad things. You may not understand karma and you may not be spiritual, but you do have enough life experience to know that when you do bad things, bad things tend to happen to you.

So the ego gets trained. It gets trained, and it gets smarter, and it actually tries to find ways around the karma. Ways to increase the darkness, which is its purpose, without being subject to the penalty or pain.

WHAT INCREASES KARMA?

Now we already know that all karma is bad, yes? But what increases karma? Well, the answer is a couple of things. Karma is controlled and increased by the choices we make. But what makes the choices? Your ego/mind makes the choices and is the actuator of karma.

You grow God by increasing darkness. Humanity chooses darkness through the ego, which is not the flesh body, but the mind. Your body is not evil. Your body is a temple, and it is the house that God lives in. You are an aspect of God, the occupant of that house.

The ego or demon or demoness (whatever works for you) – its path to ascension, to become an Angel or Spirit – is through darkness. The more darkness it brings, the larger it grows. Just as with your soul, except the opposite is true. The more light it brings in, the bigger the soul grows, but it is in putting them together (the ego and soul) that you are made whole.

The ego is the catalyst, the active ingredient and the driving force. The ego determines the amount of karma that you will receive by the choices that it makes. It, the ego/mind, creates the darkness, and then the soul must balance by bringing light to that darkness.

Now the brain comes into play a little bit there, that little 10% of brain. Remember when you are having a conversation in your head, there are two things talking, yes? It is not just one thing talking to itself. What are the two voices in your head? One is the mind/ego, and the other is the brain. The mind/ego is much more powerful because it controls 90% of your brain, whereas the brain controls only a small 10% of itself. But the brain has its say so. It actually can get in there and carry on a little conversation. It usually never wins, but it is the unconscious objector to what is happening.

The ego controls and incurs the karma by the trespasses that it makes. A trespass is a choice to incur darkness, also called a cause. Even if "you" are not consciously making that choice, the ego, which is mostly hidden from you, is making it. One way or another, the ego is going to find a way to create darkness.

AN EYE FOR AN EYE

Is the balancing of karma "eye for an eye"? No. Just because you were a murderer in the last lifetime, it does not mean that you have to be murdered in this lifetime. It is *not* "an eye for an eye" anymore. Yet all things have you been and will you be. The system ensures that, by the time you are finished here, you will have been all things human: male and female, gay and straight, rich and poor, etc.

A lot of us old souls in the old days, 5,000 years ago, were subject to this old method of "an eye for an eye." Kill and you would be killed. Michael's rule over Israel and the Angels was an "eye for an eye." All of the Angels that were Israel were subject to an "eye for an eye" justice. Trespass for trespass. They were the refiners who refined the new creation, the first souls handed out at Mount Sinai.

As the scriptures state in Jeremiah, "Jerusalem is the frying pan and you (Israel) the Angels are the meat." Understand that out of chaos comes order. Egypt was chaos (darkness) and Israel/Hebrews were order (light). Karma ensures order out of chaos. But everything has changed to a simpler, more humane, system since the new souls of Christ Michael began incarnating 2,000 years ago.

WILL AND LOVE

The vibration that is love, that is Christ, did not come into this world until Christ rose or ascended. If you go back to the Old Testament, they do not talk about love. They hardly mention the word love. The vibration of love did not come into the world until Christ's ascension. If you look at the New Testament, it is all about love. Love did not come into this world until Christ. Before Christ it was *will*, the will of the Creator. After Christ's return or ascension, love was born to this world. You had will and then love, but each in their perfect order. It was through will that love became.

This is why many unaware teachers, masters, and religious believe that the Old Testament God was a tyrant and the New Testament God is all loving. Nonsense. It was the same God. *Will became love.* Chaos became order. Darkness became light. YHVH means "to be" or "to become." It does not mean Yahweh. It is not the name of God, and it does not mean I AM. It means "to be" or "to become." Michael *became* Christ. The God of Israel *became* God of this universe. All new fragments (souls) are fragmented from him in the last 2,000 years. 1 Corinthians 12:11 – "That one and same

Spirit (Christ) dividing to every man, individually as he will."

AS SHEEP TO THE SLAUGHTER

The system overseen by Michael was "will." Will of the Father. And it was an eye for an eye. Kill and you would be killed. If you were an adversary, or carried an opposing Spirit not of YHVH, then we, the Angels, wanted to kill you the flesh. This was because, when we killed you, your spirit came out. It was then collected and placed into the whole. And that is the main reason why wars were constantly fought; to kill the bodies and recover the wealth within. It was a constant cycle of birth and death, seeding and recovering. This is how the refining process worked. We were "as sheep to the slaughter," as Scripture states.

We also were subject to death at any time. The spirit inside could only be recovered upon death of the body. The lump, or whole, was constantly increased spiritually by adding the refined material out of the flesh body which was killed to increase the whole. Death served to increase the spiritual body. Every time a new soul (fragment) came out, it was a higher vibration than the last time, since the lump or whole was constantly being raised in light.

THE EGO INCREASES KARMA

Back to the original question again, the ego determines your growth or ascension rate. And understand, the greater the darkness, the greater the light. The Creator commanded that light shine out of darkness. Why? Because darkness "is." Darkness exists in this world, and light comes from above this world, and they have to be in balance. So you have some egos that are big and tough and strong and have incarnated a lot. The point being that the bigger, stronger, and older you are, the more darkness you have experienced and overcome. You have created it for you to experience and to overcome. It is in the overcoming that you become.

OUT OF DARKNESS COMES LIGHT

2 Corinthians 4:6 – "For God commanded the light to shine out of darkness." Thus said, you have to understand that your path back to the Creator is through darkness. Out of that darkness comes light. *There is no other way*. And this is where many fail to understand the Creator's system. Understand, the better you (the ego) do your job, the sooner the reward and the greater the reward, through greater or fewer incarnations. Your ego determines or earns your karma. It governs the level of karma, the amount of karma, and the measure of darkness. Its purpose is to create as much darkness as it can. Why? Because its ascension is determined by the amount of darkness generated, requiring the soul to balance with light.

Hopefully you now understand how you incur karma. You do not have to go out and shoot somebody, kill somebody, or beat somebody up. Thinking about it is enough. Planning, plotting, and scheming to do harm, still incurs karma.

SOUL AND EGO ARE ALWAYS BALANCED

It is a choice, and the greater the darkness, the greater the measure of light. This is why it is said (the Bible says this also), and it is a spiritual law – nothing bad can happen to you that you are not prepared to deal with. Why is that?

Because you are always in balance between darkness and light. The evil you place upon yourself is balanced by the light you also call to yourself. You, the soul, are always equal to you, the ego, because you are balanced between light and dark. So nothing bad can happen to you that you are not prepared to deal with. It is a standoff. Your soul can bring as much light as your little demon (ego) can bring darkness.

So the ego is the actuator and driving force for your ascension. The answer to the question is *the ego*. The ego increases your karma through choices, which result in intentional trespasses and darkness.

WHO IS IN CHARGE OF DISPENSING MY KARMA TO ME?

Your ego creates, dispenses, and causes you to incur the karma. Your ego controls the level of karma (darkness) that it places upon itself (you) in various amounts depending upon the trespass.

God does not give you your karma. Your Angel does not give you your karma. The neighbor does not give you your karma. You do it for (or to) yourself. You are in complete control of your own ascension through the amount of karma you earn and then clear. It is automatic. The choices that you make determine the level of darkness that you will experience.

YOUR PATH IS UNIQUE

Everybody's life path is different. Why? Because of choices, which regulate karma. This is why no one is at the same level of awareness, spiritually speaking. I am a 33. Siriliel is a 33. Ankaaraa is a 33. Are we all the same? No. The amount of darkness that you have been subject to has determined your amount of light and thereby your vibrational level. Take a group of 11's - none of them are the same. A group of 5 walk-ins - none of them are the same. A group of 4's - none of them are the same. Even those at similar soul levels are all slightly different because the life path is designed and created by you. This is quite important.

Although all of us come from one and the same Creator, or Source, we are all unique because of our unique paths back to the Creator, which is determined by our choices. Each choice affects the path or return back to the Creator. No two life paths are the same, because nobody's choices are the same. No ego makes the same choices as somebody else, because each one is different. Each path back to the Creator is unique. It is your path. You build it, and you create it. So the ego dispenses the karma to itself. You govern and determine your own level of Godliness or ascension.

"Aren't we also fragments of the planetary ego? So don't we, as egos, play off of each other as well? It's not purely an individual process."

Yes, your ego/mind is a fragment of the planetary ego, a.k.a. Spirit of the World. But *your* ego determines *your* growth for *you.* Nobody else determines your level of refinement but you. You choose the level of darkness that you bring upon yourself by the trespass that you commit. It can be a thought, as in, "You are a jerk," or a physical act, like driving to someone's house and keying his car. There are two main levels of trespass (even three as we mentioned earlier), but each are trespasses. The thought, or mental trespass, brings on a smaller amount of darkness, but the direct act is a whole other level of darkness.

THE MENTAL TRESPASS

Master egos are skilled at increasing darkness without a direct trespass. Remember, the ego learns, after lifetimes of pain, through the acts of direct trespasses (face to face) and thereby suffering the karma from the direct trespass. The ego finds ways to increase the darkness without incurring major trauma or punishment to itself (the physical body). The ego grows, and becomes a master of incarnation and reincarnation.

The mental thought trespass is what most older/mature egos use to create the darkness, since the more serious direct trespass calls for a direct cleanse. In other words, a face to face trespass requires a face to face cleanse. Remember, the effect of the karma is carried out on the flesh body. The ego does not want to suffer the consequences, so it gets smarter.

EGOS WORK TOGETHER

Angels work together as groups, but demons work together even more so. You determine your karma, nobody else. But there are those people in your life who help you to bring out the darkness. Your wife may make you so darned upset that you go out and commit some trespass against somebody else, but you are still responsible for the act. In fact, a lot of times loved ones play a very big part, not only working off karma between each other, but causing each other to incur karma. Do not think that one demon (ego/mind) does not talk to another one, saying, "Hey, help me out here! Get me riled up so I can go out and create some havoc!" Do not think it doesn't happen, because it does. And in any coming together of egos (people), three things can happen: light and dark are exchanged, light and light are exchanged, or dark and dark are exchanged.

HOW DO WE INCUR KARMA?

We already covered this, but in the interest of clarity let's state it again briefly and elaborate a little further. We incur karma through a trespass, and usually it is an intentional trespass against another human, not an animal. I think the karma should be ten times worse when you commit a trespass against an animal; when you take advantage of a poor dog, a cat, a mouse, anything. My God, especially if it is intentional! But karma only applies to human interaction.

THOUGHTS AND ACTIONS

When you incur karma against another human it can be a thought or an action. Remember, thought trespasses are not as bad as intentional actions, such as a trespass against the flesh. In other words, like I said in an earlier example, I can think bad things, and I will not incur as much karma. But I can also go and steal someone's car and create a lot more karma.

Every negative thought directed at a person incurs karma. Intent matters too. It is an enforcement of will to create a gain or a lust or a deception, and it can come in any way, shape, or form. Most people earn most of their karma with thoughts. That is the easiest way for an ego to create karma – thinking bad thoughts about another person. And I want you to understand all of these so that you are aware of what is happening when you are making choices and reacting to other people.

Here is an example of how it works. I am driving down the road. You are not paying attention and you drift over into my lane. I start honking the horn and say, "#!@% you." With that I've already incurred karma. I have caused darkness by creating negative thought forms against another person.

By the way, the easiest way to increase darkness, without taking too much retribution, is through thoughts rather than direct actions.

KARMA AFFECTS QUALITY OF LIFE

Karma affects the quality of the incarnation from those who prosper to those who suffer. Darkness, while necessary for the growth of both ego and soul, and thereby the Creator, ensures that refining or balancing is required. One's darkness must be overcome. It is during the overcoming that the quality of the human life diminishes. Sometimes full attention must be given to overcoming great darkness, and as a result, all business, family, and health-related issues are put aside. Some have called this the dark night of the soul, yet those who incur and clear great karma experience many dark nights of the soul.

DARKNESS DRAWS YOU IN

Let me divulge a great secret about this. I have heard many people say, "We see evil people all of the time, and it seems as if nothing happens to them. There is no punishment." Here is what you must understand. When you are increasing karma and gaining darkness, your life is usually going quite well. As you incur karma or darkness against you, it is usually just after you have been filled with light. You feel like a new man or woman. And what does a new man do? Seek additional darkness!

BALANCING WITH LIGHT CAN BE DIFFICULT

The valleys in your life are created when the soul is balancing the body with light. These are the low times. While karma is being increased, life in the body is at its best. The bad times come upon you when you are balancing the darkness with light. Remember, all karma is not balanced on a one-to-one ratio. The life cycle is composed of climbs and plateaus. You ascend (climb) spiritually when you are acquiring karma. You plateau or level off while you are balancing (clearing) karma. Once balanced you climb again. There are extended periods of increasing darkness as determined by the ego in younger souls (those incarnate in the 1-9 numbers). Sometimes the ego is not willing to subject itself to balancing (it is avoiding karma), and continues seeking and enjoying the good life in the flesh body. Pain is then brought to bear to force the ego to stop and allow the balancing by light.

THE MODERATE PATH

There comes a time when the younger egos eventually find that it is much easier, and much less painful, to give and take more gradually. The unwillingness to subject the flesh body to balancing by light eventually brings pain. The great ride comes to a halt, and disease and illness can occur. Then a longer period of time is required to balance the body with light (dark night of the soul).

HOW DO WE REDUCE KARMA?

To review briefly, there are two different types of karma in effect. There are those that incur it in the 1 through 9 cycle (a lifetime behind) and those who are Masters (on instant karma). It is much easier for Master vibrations, and those of us who are a little more spiritually aware, knowing that our ascension and our spiritual level are no longer determined through darkness. So you do not need to grow the darkness any longer. As an aware spiritual being, one needs to become more directly conscious of what incurs karma (and we have gone through that).

MAKE BETTER CHOICES

So, knowing how the system works, why it exists and what it is used for, the simple answer is: make better choices. Remember, the choice creates the cause. Through knowledge I give you power to overcome yourself. Thus said, it is possible to reduce the amount of incarnations by reducing the amount of karma incurred and the required clearing. It's simple stuff really.

Imagine if humanity, as a collective ego, realized and understood how karma works, and that there are two main options. What if the individual egos, now aware of the mental trespass that Master vibrations use, could begin to create darkness through mental instead of physical trespasses? How much violence and hardship could be lessened in society? Feel into it. Think if you must.

You have to understand that, for most of humanity, choices come through the mind, a.k.a. the ego. In reality you do not have any free will. You have been taught that you have free will; however, you really do not, because the ego makes the choices it wants to make. And understand that those choices are in the ego's best interest. They are not random choices. The brain is not making them.

USE THE MIND OF GOD

When you can begin to choose with the Mind of God, which is the soul, which is in the heart center, you take the ego out of the picture and out of the power seat. You normally use the mind for everything. For thinking, acting, writing, eating and understanding. Yet you must learn to use the Mind of God, the heart center.

Whenever you use the mind (thinking) to make the choices and decisions, you are giving your power away to the ego, and that power is going to darkness. Yet this is what the ego does and this is what it is supposed to do.

When you start to feel through the heart center, everything begins to change. It is the hardest thing in the world to do, because your mind is screaming at you, and pressing every button there is. It will cause fear, panic, and anxiety. It will scream at you, "Don't trust it! Don't trust it! I am the one. You know that is wrong. Trust me. How can you listen to the heart? That doesn't make any sense! Common sense tells you that."

Remember, the ego deals with rationality, reason and common sense. How can you go with a feeling over the common-sense thing to do? We usually disregard the feeling and go with the common-sense thing 99.9% of the time. We all do it. Why? Because the ego, logical as it is, convinces us that feelings can't be trusted. It is also because we confuse the heart center feelings with emotions, yet they are not the same.

LEARN TO TRUST THE HEART

When you first start using the heart center it is very difficult. But the more you do it and hold off the ego, you find that the outcome of using the heart center was correct, and the more confident you get and the more willing you are to try it again. After a while you begin to reduce the grip that the mind has over your actions. The ego's grip on you has been reduced. It allows itself to reduce itself. But the only way to control karma is to make better choices. You must be aware that you are caught up in a game. You don't make the choices, something else does.

This is very hard to do when you are incarnated as a 1 through 9 soul. Suppose you are a 7, and your number/path is spirituality, and you are just starting to learn how to be spiritual. The ego is much more powerful and has almost complete control of everything. So there is almost no power at all or awareness of the entire picture.

BECOME CONSCIOUS OF YOUR CHOICES

It gets down to choices, and choices have outcomes. From every choice there is a consequence. Create your own reality by the choices you make in your life. You have to understand where those choices are being made; in the ego/mind, not in the heart center and not by your brain. And it needs to be that way. God needs you to make mistakes so that he and you both grow. You lose, and he wins. But every time you lose, and overcome it, you are grown. So, in essence, it is a win-win for all involved; ego, soul, and Creator.

GOD WINS EITHER WAY

I think Shawn and I have explained this a lot of times to a lot of people; that no matter what, the Creator wins. Again, if you make a good choice, it is God's gain, and if you make a bad choice, he actually gains even more.

BE THE LOVE WHEREVER YOU ARE

Every one of you has to be so conscious of your choices when it comes to people. When anything comes into your mind about another person, no matter what it is, be the love, be the love. Force yourself to be the love. You cannot lose with love. *Be the love wherever you are.* Through this you shine your light into the darkness of the world around you.

OVERCOME THE EGO BY NOT USING IT

You are grown by your choices. I came to understand at an early age that, from all the darkness and bad choices I made, pain followed. I learned that if I do "x," then "y" happens. We learn much the way a dog does, through positive and negative reinforcement. Again, the ego controls the choices. To control karma one must choose from the heart center, which is to take the ego out of play.

It sounds simple and it's great advice, but it is the hardest thing for humanity to do. Understand, you cannot reduce ego or get rid of ego, and you cannot directly overcome your ego through some kind of force. It sits in the power seat. It *is* the active force. You think through it, and it controls all five senses, and through it comes all of your individual understanding, logic, and reason.

The only way to overcome the ego is to not use it. In order to accomplish this, one must learn to think through the heart center, the Mind of God.

"If we did that, we wouldn't have all these challenges, would we?"

Yes, but then again, if we all did it, we wouldn't grow, because we would do everything correctly. Strange as it may sound, God does not grow through correct action. That is why we have the ego. We need the drama and the darkness so we can overcome them. Through this overcoming of darkness we grow. Understand that while we can never overcome our egos, we can and must overcome the darkness that our egos create.

YOU MUST OVERCOME YOURSELF

Remember what the Bible says: "To those that overcome I will give." What you are overcoming is your karma, your darkness. But what are you *really* overcoming? You are overcoming *yourself.* You are overcoming the obstacles that *you* have created. You, the ego, create the obstacles, and you, the soul, overcome them. How? By bringing light. You, the ego, create darkness, and you, the soul, overcome that darkness. This is what happens, and this is what your life is all about. It never stops; obstacle, obstacle, and obstacle.

If you stop and examine your life with total honestly, you will see that you created your own obstacles throughout your entire lifetime, and you overcame them.

WHAT HAPPENS WHEN WE INCREASE KARMA AND WHEN WE DECREASE KARMA?

When you increase karma, what have you done? You have increased darkness. If you have increased karma then you have increased darkness.

So, how do you decrease your karma? You balance it with light. You do not actually decrease the karma. It does not make the karma smaller, it removes it. Through balancing, it is removed and transmuted. The gain is taken from your body and stored in the Astral.

You incur karma and you balance it your entire lifetime. For a 1 through 9, not the Master vibrations, they incur karma now, and they balance it later. And the Master vibrations incur karma and balance it almost immediately.

Do you understand what is happening? You grow, and you grow, and you grow. Every time you bring light to darkness, you have grown. The creation has grown because the Creator is both polarities. When darkness grows, he grows. When light grows, he grows also.

"Peaks and valleys and plateaus" is a good way of describing the way we incur and balance karma. The soul grows in peaks and valleys. Actually, you climb and then plateau. By growing the darkness you are climbing, and then you will plateau until you are balanced, as light is sent. Then you will climb again.

The climbing is the growing of darkness. The plateau is the balancing with light. It is as if there is a pause, or waiting period, in your physical life that all people go through.

So you climb, climb, and climb; this is the increase of darkness. Light is brought, and you plateau. You balance during the plateau, and then you grow again. You are balancing throughout your entire life. Grow darkness and balance with light; grow darkness and balance with light; grow darkness and balance with light. This is how it works.

"It sounds like the cosmic stock market to me. The shares go up and they go down, it's peaks and troughs."

It's more like peaks and plateaus; up and then level off, up and then level off. But understand that you are not going backwards, you are increased. Every time that you grow darkness, and light is then sent, you have become bigger. If you have been balanced, you have become bigger. Each time you have become bigger, the Creator has become bigger also, right? The fragment or seed that you are grows, and so does the whole, a.k.a. the Creator.

LIGHT CAN DO NOTHING BY ITSELF

This process happens in small increments, lifetime through lifetime through lifetime. The darkness, you could say, is the food for the light. The light can do nothing of itself.

Get this. In order for the soul to overcome, there must be that which *can* be overcome. As the soul is passive, it can only hope that you will excel at creating karma/darkness for it. For of its own self it can do nothing.

CONTAINERS OF LIGHT AND DARKNESS

You can look at the flesh body as an empty glass. It is continuously filled by both ego and soul. The darkness generated by the ego is placed into the flesh body (empty glass). The soul brings light from above and also places it into the flesh body. The flesh body is the container (glass) in which both darkness and light is stored. First darkness is added and then light is sent to balance. Both the darkness and the light placed into the body are essentially spirit, since both come from Source. Remember, the Creator is the light *and* the dark.

Your body is like a mini water (spirit) treatment center. It is the smaller container that both darkness and light are mixed, or purified, in. This mixture is then carried up and placed into the larger container in the Astral, and placed under your account as you, where it is further processed.

The creation is *you*, and it is your contribution which is stored on your books in the Astral. This is what you continually grow and refine through all of your incarnations. However, each time this happens you gain and retain an amount of the transmuted "water" (spirit), and carry that within the flesh body. So above (the Astral you) and below (the physical you) are also in balance. This process continues day by day, month by month, incarnation after incarnation.

YOU WILL BECOME A GREAT LIGHT

This is how spirit is grown through your flesh and why each incarnation you become larger and larger, purer and purer (more refined) until your light has become equal to the pure light which comes from the Celestial realm. This is the only way to enter the Celestial realm, by matching presence or light or vibration.

Through incarnation and the balancing of karma, the seed sown in darkness (you) will become a great light.

HOW DOES KARMA AFFECT US?

A) You cannot directly serve the Creator, he cannot directly manifest to you, with existing karma. We explained this in detail earlier in the book.

B) Your entire cycle of incarnations is all about achieving your goal, to work off and balance karma. You do this by bringing light to darkness, by balancing darkness with light. In so doing you grow yourself and the Creator.

KARMA REQUIRES MORE INCARNATIONS

Karma is darkness on your books. Darkness is the cause and the effect is light. What is caused in the flesh has its effect in the spirit. There are those with heavy, heavy, heavy karma; some who cannot achieve balance in one lifetime and instead require several lifetimes to achieve balance. They could be, let us say, a 7. They could repeat that 7 lifetime over and over until they are ready for the 8 cycle, and have balanced all of the previous karma.

KARMA CAN AFFECT QUALITY OF LIFE

In times of great unbalanced karma or darkness, the quality of human life is diminished. The focus of both ego and soul is to balance. The focus is not on the family financial situation or any other Earthly endeavor. It is the plateau period, as I have mentioned, and all experience this during the lifetime.

THE SOUL SEES THE NEXT LIFETIME

The soul, when in the Astral, actually sees the next incarnation. Now, nothing is predestined. Anyone that says it is predetermined or predestined is mistaken. There is no predestination. It is cause and effect, cause and effect; choice and outcome, choice and outcome.

There is only one thing predetermined: the Creator always wins, always grows, always gains. Why? Because he is all there is. There is nothing in his way. No obstacles other than himself. The Creator can be compared to a chess player moving both sides of the board. He always wins no matter which side of the board he wins from.

So you, the soul, see your upcoming lifetime. In that next lifetime, your first purpose is to balance karma. You will have the opportunity, for instance, to see that this one lifetime will balance all existing karma. It may be an incarnation of starvation in Africa, it may be living a lifetime full of pain, or it may be an early termination. Is this the incarnation that you want to take? You have that option.

Maybe you are shown a lifetime in which you will balance x-amount of karma. Or you are shown one that is the slow road. With that option it might take two or three more lifetimes to balance the existing karma. You might say, "OK, I will take that one." But not all souls are equal. Not all souls come from the same Archangel. They do not all come from the same place and not all stand up and take what they have earned, believe me.

DO FREE WILL AND KARMA GO TOGETHER?

Yes, they do. Free will, karma, and reincarnation, as I explained, actually go together. There really is no free will, and I am not supposed to tell you that because "God gave us free will." But you don't have free will. It is a royal scam. You cannot have free will when you, the real you, is not making the choice.

What makes the choice? The only thing that can make the choice is the mind, the ego, the demon, or demoness. Your brain doesn't make the choice, your soul doesn't make the choice. The ego makes the choice. And what is the ego's purpose? To create darkness or drama.

So if the ego's only objective and purpose in its ascension is based upon creating more darkness, and "it" is making the choices, what type of choice is it going to make every time? The ego will make a dark choice every time. That is the only choice it *can* make.

So in reality you do not have free will. You do not because the ego is making the choice for its best interest. When two jobs are offered to you, where one pays $10,000 per year and one pays $20,000 (and the tasks are equal), which one are you going to choose? You will choose the one with more money, of course. The ego does the same thing. It chooses for its best interest. Now, is it going to make a choice that is going to increase light or increase darkness? Let me see, I am the ego. If I am going to make a choice to increase light, what good does that do for me? Nothing. But if I make a choice that increases darkness, I get a reward. What am I going to choose? Whatever gets me the reward, of course, which, for the ego, is darkness.

As I mentioned above, the only predetermined outcome is that the Creator always wins, since he moves (and is) all of the pieces as he sees fit. He empowers the ego and the soul, each with specific and opposing purposes, to grow him.

Do you understand that you do not have free will? People tend to confuse "freedom of choice" with free will. You have choices available, but you do not have free will. Free will and freedom of choice are two different things. Free will is the ability to choose light (or God) over darkness or evil. That is free will. Freedom of choice is Burger King or McDonalds, the beach or skiing, sex or no sex, steak or spaghetti – that is freedom of choice. The free will that you believe you have is choosing good over evil, light over dark, God over whatever. You do not even have that. The game is rigged.

That which is doing the choosing is biased and gets its reward by choosing darkness. Because the greater the darkness, the greater its reward.

YOU MUST APPEAR TO HAVE FREE WILL

So understand that there is no free will, but you have to appear to have free will, to make it seem fair and that you have the ability to choose. You will have your free will when you have learned how to take control of your power, which I will teach you. But for now, where most of us are right now, I say "be the love", "be the light", "be good"...because we are not those things. We need to *be the love*, even the Bible teaches that. We need to be the light and be the friend and be the good person, because we are not those things. And by "we" I mean the human or humanity. The soul is spotless and blameless because it is passive, but the ego will choose darkness every time. This is evident in society and within yourself, if you observe it.

Once you get to a certain level of spiritual awareness you understand that. Why? Because you have incarnated enough times and you have seen the outcome. You understand that you can choose light, yet you don't grow by choosing light first. If so, you actually become out of balance, and you cannot cheat the system. The system is slanted because you are the soul/seed that is growing. That soul is the backseat driver. It does not drive the car, it does not choose. It is the effect, not the cause. The ego is the driver of the car.

LOVE AND LIGHT ARE HALF OF THE TRUTH

Many in the spiritual movements, both Eastern and Western, teach love and light, etc., etc. And I love being loved. I love love. Yet they are only teaching half of the truth. It is evil and darkness which bring love and light. The people who teach love and light – that's great, it is all good stuff. But, through ignorance of God, they are actually hindering themselves and all those who listen. If all you are doing is focusing upon bringing the light (unless you are a direct servant of God and he has put you in the position to do that) you are moving out of the system that grows you.

You then get those that are over-balanced toward the light. They are so goofy and out of balance because they are so drawn to one side. So their growth is stopped, and they stop being able to serve the Creator and themselves, because they are out of balance. Sooner or later they are going to have to bring great darkness upon themselves to balance it out.

So understand what I said and how it works. Free will goes hand in hand with choices and outcomes. It is the allowing of being free to choose (although you are not really choosing) that sets the stage for the game. When you choose darkness, which is guaranteed, then light is sent to balance.

So free will, incarnation, and reincarnation go hand in hand with karma. You incarnate to gain karma, and you reincarnate to remove karma. And free will allows you to choose good over bad, light over dark, God over whatever. And yet the ego always guarantees that you will choose darkness, no "ifs," no "ands," and no "buts."

THE CREATOR IS THE ONLY CHOICE

And remember, no matter what choice you are making or what you *think* you understand; you likely don't. In choosing evil, because you are evil or enjoy the dark or think you are some sort of rebel, it's not quite as you think. In choosing light, because you believe that you are good and all lovey dovey, you are not. Each choice, in the Creator's eyes, is correct, light or dark. Why? Because the only choice is him. There is no other choice but him. Nothing else exists.

If you choose red, it's him. If you choose blue, it's him. If you choose steak or fish, it's him. If you choose darkness and evil, or light and love – yes, both are him. The Creator is the only choice possible, because he is all there is. In that sense, there is no free will because every choice is him. There is no other option or choice possible.

"I have been half way to a bad thought and I have caught myself thinking it. Have I incurred karma? I am half way through the act, but I have caught myself."

That is really an awesome question. You see, that is why I love questions and thoughts from others. That is the first step in being able to create your own reality – being able to catch the ego at its task.

That is like taking the first baby step; being able to catch yourself, your ego, in mid-trespass. So, in the middle of the negative thoughts, you caught yourself making them, right? But you did not allow yourself to continue with the trespass?

"Yes. I do it quite often. For example, when one of my children has acted up and pushed my buttons and I trespass."

That is what they are supposed to do, by the way. As I said, egos work together to create darkness and karma. They play off of each other, and they incarnate together to work off karma and to incur karma between themselves. Yes, of course, your family members are the actuators of your little demon, especially when it is hungry. They are getting the demon to eat. The children cause the situation for you to create the drama. That also is an example of cause and effect. They misbehave = cause. You get angry (create darkness) = effect. Your darkness then becomes another cause that will require another effect. Can you see that? It is mind boggling the web of interaction (cause and effect) that we are caught up in.

"Or maybe even my relationship with my partner. My ego loves creating drama, and I actually catch my ego creating it, and I stop."

Awesome. That is awesome, awesome, awesome. I do that all the time, especially with people close to me. They are my actuators of demon food, a.k.a. drama. For instance, I was driving to Texas, and I had this little issue with someone. The whole way there for a six hour drive my ego was working it (the anger) over and over and over, and I am thinking, "My God, stop! I let this go two nights ago. Why am I sitting here thinking about this and getting angry again; why, why, why?" Then I said, "Alfie, damn you Alfie!" (Alfie is the nickname for my ego, or demon.) Then there was just a big laugh. When the ego is hungry and needs to feed, what does it feed on? Drama and emotional energy.

It uses the past to effect the present. It constantly brings up past issues and memories of pain, to either feed itself or manipulate a situation in order to create darkness. And we, humanity, are clueless to this situation, which may occur daily, over and over. We are prisoners to our own past.

DEMON FOOD VS KARMA

Egos actually feed each other. One is hungry and, believe it or not, it calls out and says, "Hey, help me out here." And the next thing you know your kid, your husband, or your lover pushes your buttons. Family members are the best button pushers. How quickly can you get worked up when your kid misbehaves or your partner irritates you, right? "I am sorry, honey, I have got a headache. What's for dinner? I am starved. Cook something!" Yes, they can push your buttons and boom, the emotional energy and drama start up again. Drama, stress, fear, worry and other forms of emotional energy are all food for the demon.

You have to understand that there is the trespass, but there is actually demon food too, and *they are two different things*. It is okay to create the drama as long as it does *not* have a controlling effect on the other person. In other words, if your son does something wrong and gets you all worked up, he is actually trespassing against you. You have not trespassed against him. And yet, both egos (demons) have been fed by the drama created through the interaction.

All karma is demon food, but not all demon food incurs karma. Likewise, all karma is darkness, but not all darkness is karma.

CATCHING YOURSELF

When you are catching yourself in mid-act of committing a trespass, then I will tell you, you are on your way. I catch myself all the time.

Remember, as a Master or a walk-in, we are subject to instant karma, so we are always going to be balancing. It could be a blow to the knee or a trip and fall. It is not going to be a crippling injury usually; you are not going to break your leg, because they are small trespasses. But regardless, it is feeding the ego.

When you are catching yourself in the middle of a trespass, shut it down and stop it. If you have not committed the entire act, then there is no karma incurred on that one.

THE EGO GROWS AS YOU GROW

It is a good thing (to catch the ego in mid act) but when you keep catching the ego, it will get craftier. It grows as you grow, and it is usually always a step ahead. In other words, as you become better at the game, the game becomes tougher. The ego becomes trickier to catch.

What is catching the ego? Do you think it is your ego catching itself? Ponder that.

"No it's my Divine self, my higher self."

Well, yes, but it is actually your brain too, and your brain gets trained. You soul is passive, remember? Your higher self (your soul) is passive, so what is catching the ego? The brain, and it also gets trained. But the ego gets trickier and smarter.

That is awesome when you can catch yourself committing an act of karma, a trespass, and stop. That is progress.

THE STRAIGHT PATH BACK

You might be tired of all this talk about karma balancing by now. Is there a quicker option? Actually, yes.

The straight path to the Creator is very simple. Get out there and give your life for another. Sacrifice yourself for another, and you can forget the whole karma cycle. Surrender yourself for another, display the highest love and you are there. Simply choose to lose. That is all it takes. I have seen many instances of it, but that is rare and is not the normal path that most take.

Giving up your physical life for the good of another, one who you do not know (it cannot be your child or a friend or relative) is the direct path to ascension. *Choose to lose.* That is the fast track, I promise you. If you are not willing to do that, and it is easier said than done (the ego will prevent it) then you play the game and you go through the system.

BE THE LOVE WHEREVER YOU ARE

We mentioned it once already, and we will mention it again, because it is important. *Be the love wherever you are.* Be the love and be the light. You don't need to be the darkness, because you already are.

Be the effect, not the cause! The soul will always bring light to darkness. This is automatic. However, you can go above and beyond. You, the creature or vessel, can demonstrate compassion for another. You can be the love, the comfort, the understanding, and the empathy, as you now know what each of us must overcome in the flesh.

The lofty task that each of you little seeds has agreed to is much more than you could ever have grasped.

IS KARMA MENTIONED IN THE BIBLE?

Yes, but they do not use the word karma. The word is "sin" in the Old Testament or "Tanakh." Sin applied to your account is karma. There are many, many passages regarding sin and the purging or refining of sin out of the Hebrews/Israel. An example from the Old Testament is this:

Isaiah 40:2 – "Speak tenderly to Jerusalem and proclaim to her that her hard service has been completed and that her sin has been paid for and that she has received double for all her sins."

But yes, it is in there, though it does not call it karma. It is called sin. It talks about it in the Old Testament and a little bit in the New Testament.

Romans 7:12 & 13 states that the law is justification of the spirit through the flesh. This was the task of Israel.

Romans 5:13 – "For until the law, sin (karma) was in the world but sin was not imputed when there was not law." Karma was not imputed until there was the individual soul from Mount Sinai (the law).

Romans 2:5 – "But according to your hardness and unrepentant heart treasure up unto yourself wrath. God, who will render every man according to his deeds (karma), tribulation and anguish upon every soul of man that does evil..."

Micah 7:13 – "The Earth (soil) will become desolate because of its inhabitants, the result of their deeds."

1 Peter 4:1 – "He that has suffered in the flesh has ceased from sin."

Through incarnation you are cleansed of sin (darkness transmuted).

DO E.T.'S AND OTHER BEINGS OR ANGELS HAVE KARMA?

Karma is applied to any human being, be they of E.T. origin or whatever. If they are incarnate on this planet in this realm, then they are subject to karma.

For those who aren't familiar with our work, there are between 5% and 15% of those incarnate that have the soul of God that could be considered "Extra-Terrestrial." However, the star systems they come from are within the firmament.

The 3D world under the firmament that we exist within was created explicitly for one purpose only: to grow the Creator through growing yourself. Anything and everything that exists in this 3D world exists to fulfill this purpose.

DIRECT AND INDIRECT SERVANTS

There is the direct servant, which is mankind, a.k.a. the flesh body, and there is the indirect servant, ordained to assist the direct servant. These are things like plants, animals, insects, trees, rivers, mountains, etc. This entire world was created to grow the Creator, and everything in it is for the benefit of mankind and to assist mankind in that growth.

Any aspect or fragment or soul of a Celestial entity, that is incarnate in this world, is subject to karma. Everything incarnate in the flesh body is subject to karma. It has to do with the soul's first purpose. Without karma there would be no growth for you, the seed/soul, and for the Creator who grows through "you."

"Nothing else in the Astral or the Celestial will have karma?"

No. Only for what is put back into the flesh. Karma cannot work without a 3D body and an ego. You must have the right polarity and the left polarity. The ego is active and the soul is passive. What creates your karma, and what balances your karma? There is only one thing that can create darkness, your ego (mind). And there is only one thing that can bring light to that darkness, the soul.

A FLESH BODY IS NECESSARY

The ego is the active catalyst to spur growth of the soul and thereby the Creator, and you must be in a flesh body for it to work. You cannot be refined or grown unless you are in a 3D body.

THE SENSES MAKE IT REAL

The senses are one key. You must see, hear, touch, taste, and smell, and it must be real. What is real for you? Only that which you have experienced through the senses. Those senses do not exist in the Astral or Celestial bodies.

SPIRIT GROWS THROUGH THE FLESH

Spirit grows itself in and through the flesh. It lives in the house. The house is the body, and you are what lives in that house. Remember always, *you are not the house; you are that which lives in the house.* Every seed/soul has to have a body.

Karma is specifically designed to grow you and the Creator automatically. Let me put it this way, it works everywhere in 3D. It governs your ascension or enlightenment (I don't like that misused word). Karma governs your growth, spiritually speaking.

WHAT IF YOU DO SOMETHING BAD TO SOMEONE BUT YOUR INTENTION IS TO HELP THEM?

Understand this first of all, there is no good karma, and there is no bad karma. There is only karma. All karma is bad. Karma is darkness applied to your account.

Now, from the Creator's point of view, karma is Divine. It serves its purpose to bring you into balance and to return you to him, automatically, by growing him and you. And he has nothing at all to do with it. You do.

Let me clarify the question. Your intent is to help somebody, but to do it you have to do something bad to them? First of all, when you trespass against another human, karma is incurred. Karma is only incurred against a person, another human, another soul incarnate. Not against an animal, not against a house, not against a car, and not against some food. Karma is a direct trespass on another person; a violation; an attempt to cheat, lie, steal, even a thought; an enforcement of will. Thinking something bad of you like "that little @#$& I would like to smack him" is a trespass, believe me. I have incurred karma because I have trespassed against you.

Thoughts are trespasses, as are direct acts. So this is a really good question. It is a higher level question that only somebody with some awareness would come up with. But if your intent is to help them by hurting them, then you are placing yourself as Creator God, and you are not that, so it is still a trespass.

Remember, even Christ did not help everyone. There were those that he would not help. He was unwilling to interfere with their karma. Understand that to interfere with one's karma is to interfere with their personal ascension, since each person's karma governs their ascension (return) to the Creator.

Any attempt to harm, to cause uneasiness, to sway, to change, or to do anything bad to another incarnate in any way, shape, or form, is a trespass. And from that trespass you have incurred karma to yourself. This is the cause, and the outcome is the effect. That, basically, is how karma is implemented.

Darkness is the cause and light is the effect; so you have increased darkness. By incurring karma you have incurred, or increased, darkness. Even if your intent was to help them, the trespass has increased darkness on your account.

Again, understand that *what is caused in the flesh has its effect in the spirit*. That is why this world we exist within was created; to grow the Creator, the All in All, through growing the smaller parts of him (you).

IS KARMA INCURRED ON THE INTENT
OR ON THE RESULT?

It's both. The thought or intent is a trespass. However, the actual act itself is a greater trespass. Both are causes, yet the effects of each trespass are different. Each type incurs a different amount of darkness.

Just to clarify that again, there are two types of trespasses. There is the *thought* trespass, which does *not* involve a physical act or a face-to-face interaction with another person. And there is a *direct* trespass, which *does* involve a physical act and/or a face-to-face encounter with at least one other human being.

Everything gets down to intent. For example, you are driving down the street and you reach down to adjust the radio, you look up, and there is a person standing in front of your car and you smacked them. Did you incur karma?

No, no karma was incurred, because it was an accident. You looked down to adjust your radio, you looked up, there he was, and you couldn't stop. It was *not* an intentional act. Karma requires an intentional act, an intentional trespass. If it was an accident, an unintentional act, then no karma was incurred on your part. However, in the scheme of things, you could have been the instrument for the other person's karma.

Let's try a different version of the same situation. You are driving down the road, and you have had a couple of beers. You are also speeding and you are not paying attention. You look up and there is somebody there, and whack, you hit them. Is it a trespass?

Yes, it was a trespass. You were no longer innocent under those conditions. You are responsible because of your bad choices. There was no need to be drinking and speeding and also not paying attention on top of it. Your bad choices contributed to the situation. Your choices effected an outcome.

Consider road rage. I am driving down the road, and somebody flips me off. So I speed up, and I turn my car, and I run them off the road. That is a direct or "face-to-face" trespass. There are accidental trespasses, those without intent, and there are intentional trespasses that I've described above.

But again, back to the original question. If you are trying to mould somebody, or shape somebody, and trespass against them to get them to do something (enforce your will for any reason), then that is a straight out trespass, even if you think it is for their own good. Because, remember, *their* karma is decided by *them*. They decide what is for their own good. If you try to make that decision for them, then you are playing God. You are interfering with God's process. Your ego decides what is right for you, and the same goes for others. You cannot impose your will on another person, even if it is done out of love.

Karma has nothing to do with the law of attraction, nothing to do with "you reap what you sow," and nothing to do with the law of cause and effect. Karma is the Divine system that keeps balance in this world under the firmament, and ensures that, sooner or later, each and every person will ascend (return) to the Creator. Karma grows God by growing "you."

HOW DOES OUR LIFE PATH NUMBER
RELATE TO KARMA?

Life path and birth path are the same thing. We've already covered how your number affects whether you are subject to regular karma or instant karma. But we can elaborate briefly on that.

Each number in the cycle denotes a different expression or experience.

One is Self
Two is Reflection
Three is Communication
Four is Work
Five is Change
Six is Family
Seven is Spirituality
Eight is Wealth and Power
Nine is Completion

These are the areas where your karma comes from and is earned.

So, for instance, three is in the area of communications, this is where your karma is incurred and cleared. Four is work, so this is where your karma is incurred and cleared. Five is change, six is family, and these are the areas where karma is incurred and cleared.

In our radio shows we've sometimes mentioned a book on numerology, by Javane & Bunker. If you are interested in more information on the subject, then get it. It's called *Numerology and the Divine Triangle*. It is the best book on numerology out there.

You can actually do the letters in your name and convert them into numbers. When you do this you will find that some numbers are missing. You may be missing sixes, or fours, or threes, those are the areas where your karma lies, in the missing numbers. You can find out exactly where it lies. It is not important to someone on instant karma because you do not have it. But each incarnation or cycle, any number from 1 through 9, works off karma in those particular areas.

THE SPIRIT IS GIVEN FOR PROFIT

(A conversation from "Allfaaraa Live" on BlogTalkRadio.)

SHAWN: I hope that everyone is directly considering the information that we teach here, especially the stuff on the ego and the soul, because it applies directly to our every day experience. I hope people are feeling into and considering and realizing, in their own experience, what is going on with those things, even though some of it is historical and does not necessarily apply to us today. What I'm saying is that this stuff is either real for you or it isn't. You either know it is, or you don't. Don't just hear something and either believe it or push it aside, without a full consideration. Don't just hear that the ego is dark, or hear that you are thinking through a larger consciousness. Don't hear these things and just believe them or reject them. This stuff is close to you and is what you are living every day. Don't just say, "Oh the ego is dark and it is over there and it is causing me to do something," and then put the blame off on something called an ego that you don't understand. I mean, you are the one that does what you do every day, and you are the one thinking through your ego. So this is something that is right there close to you...it's YOU (or is functioning as you). Take responsibility for it. Don't just hear it with your mind and believe something we say, without actually realizing for yourself how it applies to your daily experience. When you assemble the pieces yourself, observing yourself and your life and the world around you, you will realize certain things directly, and this is when it becomes real for you.

ALLFAARAA: Sure, but which "you" are you talking about?

You are saying you, but which you are you talking about? You are the soul, the seed that grows. It is the ego, which is also you, which makes you believe that you are the body. So when you want to blame evil on your evil ego, it is you also! It just happens to be a larger consciousness that you think through, but it is still you. You cannot blame anything or anyone else, ok? You are the evil, and humanity is the evil. The soul is the light, the good. There is no evil/darkness in the soul. It is grown through evil, but you, the ego, are the evil that exists in this world, and that is how it is supposed to be. There is nobody else to blame. You, the ego, are the darkness, just as you, the soul, are the light.

SHAWN: Right, I agree. So anyway, we want to continue with the subject of karma. We covered a lot of questions. We covered most of the standard questions in the previous chapters like "What is karma?" We tried to straighten some of that out, but now we want to finish those questions.

ALLFAARAA: Let us keep going. Here are some new assessments that have been coming to me recently.

One of the things that you could say about karma is that it is almost like God's fertilizer. Karma is the fertilizer that causes the creation (you) to grow, if you want to look at it that way. The more darkness that is grown, the more overcoming that is required in this current lifetime, and the more light is sent to balance. Does that make sense to you, Shawn?

SHAWN: Yes.

ALLFAARAA: Pretty basic stuff. Karma is darkness. That

darkness stimulates the growth, or the light, of the soul, does it not?

SHAWN: Yes, it must.

ALLFAARAA: So basically you can look at karma as God's fertilizer. That is another way to look at it. Because the system in this world, this little test tube world (and again "this world" means under the firmament), was created solely to create (increase) God through creating (increasing) yourself.

SHAWN: We could look at it like stimulation, almost like pain.

ALLFAARAA: Karma is fertilizer. Let's not look at pain as fertilizer because we are all subject to pain, but we don't want it. And we don't need it. We don't have to deal with the pain. Everything I have been teaching you is to grow God without pain; to achieve your purpose without suffering. To bring light to darkness without pain and suffering.

SHAWN: Ok, good point.

ALLFAARAA: Alright, now let's go over something else I want to cover quickly. Some of the questions in this book may appear simple or stupid or repetitive. But we are leaving them in here and answering them because I want to be as clear as possible. If a question comes to one of my student's minds then it will also come to someone else out there, so we might as well answer whatever we can.

Now here is something one must understand, the soul

chooses the lifetime. Those that wish to increase (grow) faster choose the hardest most difficult lifetimes. There are several options presented when you reincarnate, because it is all based on time. The current or preferred lifetime available now and/or the next incarnation could be 50 to 80 years later, but it is all the same time, as there is no time above. So you can choose how fast you want to become and return to God, to return to the Celestial. You choose the lifetime, and the most difficult incarnation is the one where you remove all of the karma incurred from the last lifetime, in the current lifetime. You balance all past karma in one lifetime. This is the most difficult incarnation and few choose this option, but it is always available and offered as the first choice, so to speak.

Understand, karma is not "dispensed." Nobody dispenses your karma. You are the creator of your own karma. You incur it, you are the dispenser, and you are the remover or balancer. It is a self-administered system and nobody else is involved. Nobody else is involved! You control the pace of your own ascension or return to the Creator. The great thing about karma is that there is no Archangel, no God and no Lord that oversees the project. You manage yourself. You choose the rate of your own ascension or return to the Creator by incurring karma and balancing that karma that you incur. And each time this is done, you grow and the Creator does also. As we have stated again and again, *you create yourself above through the flesh below*. As you are growing the "you" above, you are also growing the Creator.

The number of lifetimes necessary to return to where you came from is dependent upon the clearing or removing of karma. The final cycle, which is the 9 series of incarnations, is completed when all of your incurred karma is totally cleared or balanced with light. Until your past and current karma is cleared/balanced, you are not finished. Only karma free can you enter the Celestial realms. This is because, through incarnation and the balancing of karma, you have achieved the frequency (light) allowing your entry, vibrationally speaking, into the upper realm. It is also because the darkness that is on your books can not be brought into the realms of light. You also will have the choice to continue in form on the Earth as a direct servant to the Creator, as a Master vibration.

SHAWN: It is hard for us to imagine because we think that there is someone out there causing the whole karma situation and so...

ALLFAARAA: There is someone...you! You are causing the whole karma situation. There is no overseer. You oversee and manage your own business. You are an independent contractor, as I have told you. God is a business owner, the biggest one that there is. His business is what, Shawn?

SHAWN: Spirit.

ALLFAARAA: Spirit, exactly. You are an independent contractor. He supplies you the product...get this in your head...and you grow it, and either you profit or lose from it. Romans 12:7 – "The Spirit is given for profit." Is that clear enough for you? What if you do not increase that Spirit? Simple, you are removed, fired, and a replacement is found. It goes back to the Bible, Romans 12 – "The Spirit is given for profit." That should say it all to you. The Spirit is given for profit, say it with me three times. The Spirit is given for profit, the Spirit is given for profit, the Spirit is given for profit. Write this on your minds and in your heart. The Spirit is given for profit.

And as to the "kicked out" part, see Matthew 25:14, the parable of the workers. If you read it you will see that, of the workers that were given the Spirit to increase, two of them increased or returned a profit and they were rewarded. One did nothing; he returned the original measure of Spirit. What happened? All that he had was taken from him and then given to one of the others who had increased the Spirit.

I hear this question often, "Oh, what am I supposed to do with my Spirit?" First, understand that you don't *have* a Spirit. You *are* a fragment (soul) of a Spirit. Essentially you are a seed that is placed into soil (flesh) that grows when it is fertilized by darkness. But, anyway, the answer is: Grow it. Increase it. You are increasing yourself. That's what you are here to do. Increase. Become. Once again, *what is caused in the flesh has its effect in the spirit.*

For incarnations (lifetimes) in the 1-9 cycle, *between* incarnations you exist in the Astral. And when it is time to reincarnate again, you will have a choice. There is the fast road to ascension, the direct path, the blue path to Michael, or there are other options available.

We'll go over it again as we did earlier. Let's say you are a 6. You can do 6 in one lifetime or, based on the karma, you can do 6 in three lifetimes. That is why, for each incarnation, you do not go up a number every time, because you have to complete or balance that karma. You may not want to take on that great amount of darkness in one single incarnation. Few do. Do you follow what I am saying? You, the soul, have the option to spread it out over multiple lifetimes, and that is why you control your own path to ascension. I say three life options are given, but that is not always the rule. However, I have never seen, in all my time incarnate, any soul go beyond the third choice, and usually two is all that is required.

Let's move on with the great questions that we have.

WHEN DID KARMA BEGIN IN THIS WORLD?

Let's review the basics again before we continue.

As I have taught you, and the Creator has taught me, this entire world was created to grow the Creator through growing yourself. That is why we came here.

The Creator manifests in a downward cause and effect manner. What is caused in the flesh has its effect in the Spirit. To affect your Spirit above, you/it must be incarnate below. The Spirit grows only in (and through) the flesh body.

Karma, as applied to the individual, started at one particular time. Previous to that there was what is called group or collective karma, because those of us who were participating then were all old Spirits/souls, fragmented from the many different Gods which existed, or were Gods ourselves. Our karma was collective, which means it was attached to that from which we were cut. But individual karma started when we had individual souls. Those first souls, as I stated earlier, were cut (fragmented) from the whole at Mount Sinai.

THE THREE KINDS OF SOULS

There are three groups or types of souls incarnate now: growers, refiners, and feeders. These are the three basic soul groups. The growers are the oldest. Growers existed from Adam to Jacob and included the 12 Archangels and the

144,000 Angels. The refiners were all the members (Angels) of Israel and their fragment souls, placed into the bodies of the Hebrews. Essentially the 144,000 were/are growers and refiners, and the feeders are those fragmented from the new soul of Christ/Michael over the last 2,000 years.

THE WAR IN HEAVEN

The entire war in Heaven and on Earth was about collecting back, or recovering, the Spirit of the Creator God. We, the Angels, went planet to planet, system to system, and hunted down all of those who possessed, but would not return, what was not theirs to keep (the Spirit of the Creator). We destroyed the host vessel to recover the spirit within, regardless of whether it a physical flesh body type host or even a planetary host. Those that remained Spirits, Gods, or even races of extra-terrestrials then fled to the soil of the Kingdom (our planet). This was to continue their treachery, knowing that the Creator God would not allow his solid ground, his Earth, to be destroyed as we destroyed Maldek/Marduk.

As we hunted them down on this planet (the soil of the Kingdom of Heaven), we recovered much of what was lost, which we did by the killing of the various flesh bodies. These were pre-hominid, Cro-Magnon and various other animals and creatures that were available. Remember, in killing the host vessel, the spirit within returns to its original source.

EARTH CLEANSING AND THE FIRMAMENT

There was a cleansing of the soil (Earth), and then a

restructuring of the heavens and the solid ground (planet) that removed all life forms. Upon death of the form, that which was incarnate in them was released and returned to the original source. The Creator God then separated the spirit above from the spirit below (the "waters" from the "waters") by the firmament, or Rakia in Hebrew, also known as the "wall."

In Genesis, "water" is another metaphor for spirit. All of what had been taken (spirit) was now trapped in one place, below the firmament. We, the Angels who served the Creator, knew that now we would get it (the spirit) back. We also knew that what we recovered would be used as ours to increase and refine, thereby building ourselves below and our realms above. To do so, all we had to do was to kill the source, the house, the body, the vehicle, or the vessel that the spirit was contained within. In killing the body we all know what happens then. The spirit is released and returns to its original source.

The Rakia, or firmament, now prevented those below from returning to the Celestial realms, and those above the wall from descending to the planet to interfere with the creation.

OUR ADAM

We began again with your/our Adam (first person), however this time the intent was to create souls, not Gods, as had been previously created. The new soul would be a direct fragment of the Creator God and placed into form with the Creator God being in complete control of all the fragments. And to maintain control, the spirit would then be dispensed from above in the Celestial realm, which also did not happen the first time. The plan involved Michael to collect all of the spiritual wealth, or glory, contained within all forms on the Earth and return it above, back to the Celestial. In the Celestial, the Creator would once again be in control of all spiritual wealth. It didn't turn out that way. Once again, Lucifer had his say. And once again, all spirit came through him.

THE BOOK OF ENOCH

That was just a very brief overview. If you wish to read more about what happened as the War in Heaven came down to the soil, the Book of Enoch comes from the Angels viewpoint. It is also in the Bible to some extent. The Bible is actually the story of the taking back of the Kingdom of Heaven from Lucifer.

INDIVIDUAL AND COLLECTIVE KARMA

Back to the subject of karma, understand what karma does. Karma governs the refinement process, the ascension process. And it is a system not a law. Karma is not a law. That is a fallacy and New Age fiction. It is a Divine system ordained to control the growth of the creation of God and you. Karma insures that most all will ascend sooner or later.

Earlier in this chapter we were describing how we would recover the material (spirit) once it was trapped beneath the firmament. To recover it we had to kill the bodies, the hosts. So the first group, from Adam all the way down to Jacob and the 12 and the 144,000, were all growers. All Spirits (no souls yet) then incarnate were growers, expanding the consciousness.

How did we grow it? By being incarnate in the flesh body and fragmenting into first-born after first-born. Essentially, even though they were called Archangels and Angels and Spirits or "Living Souls," the system was the same. They (we) were essentially Gods, just as Christ accurately called the Hebrews in John 10:34 - "Is it not written in your law, I said ye are Gods?" A God is a Spirit that can fragment itself and place that fragment into form (flesh body), thereby increasing itself. Spiritually, the more forms one could place themselves into, the greater they became. This was the system for growth at that time in our Earthly spiritual history.

There was no karma and thereby no refinement of the individual soul, because there was no individual soul yet. There was karma of the collective, and basically every God/Spirit/Angel was a karma server too. But there was no refinement of the spiritual material being grown in the forms. Not yet anyway. All of the material had to be collected.

There was still original spirit, or raw grain, existing within those trapped beneath the firmament. All of the Nephilim were incarnate again. Egypt was the home of the Gods, and yet all of the spiritual wealth possessed in Egypt and in the Nephilim belonged to the Creator and not the various Gods who were in possession of it. This is what was left to be collected on this planet. Michael, the leader of the Angelic host, was ordained to collect it, and through his collection and his return to the Celestial, he would become Christ, Lord of the Universe. He would be dispensing all that he recovered below (spirit), from the Celestial realm above.

COLLECTING THE GROWN SPIRIT

Michael and the Angels of Israel came to collect all of this spirit by acting through the flesh bodies of the Hebrews. The Creator is passive and Michael is active, yet through the flesh body in the 3D world the Creator's will is carried out. Thus passive becomes active, through the form. Understand that you are a servant, a pawn in a game of creation. Remember, the Creator had said no more floods, no more mass cleansings. No more heavenly wars. "No longer will I kill myself for myself." This was the system in the past. Return the spirit to him by killing the host. Consider events like the flood (Noah) as well as Sodom and Gomorrah. The Creator would cast many seeds. He would then prune or clean the various lines by mass destruction of the hosts (bodies). This was the old refining process. Weed out the unripe fruit. The first mass cleansing (after Adam) was the flood, leaving only the Adamic line incarnate. The last was Sodom and Gomorrah.

THE HEBREWS IN EGYPT

The Hebrews were chosen (or created actually) for their bodies, and they grew the Spirit of the World, essentially Lucifer, in Egypt. While there, they manifested and increased it more in 9 incarnations than ever before. They spent 9 generations there to complete the cycle of 9 or 430 years. They were working the iron smelting furnaces of Egypt, growing raw grain (spirit) into low grade iron (spirit). The Hebrews were not slaves but workers; in Hebrew it's "Avadeem." They were employees or workers. "Iron," like "grain or "bronze," refers to low-grade spirit. Higher aspects of refined spirit are considered "gold" or "silver." Holy Spirit is "bread." From Isaiah 28:28 – "Grain must be ground (refined) to make bread." Raw spirit must be refined to make it holy or pure.

RECOVER THEN REFINE

So the refining process could not start until we recovered all of the wealth/spirit. And the wealth not in the Creator's possession was in Egypt, the home of the Gods, as well as various other people's that the Nephilim were incarnate within. In order to recover it we had to destroy the host vehicle, so we killed the first-born sons of all the Nephilim and those of Egypt. The first-born son contained the fragment of the originator, because it incarnated from first-born to first-born. If you killed the first-born son, and the first-born of the first-born son, there would be nowhere for the Spirit to incarnate in; no host or vessel. We also killed the first-born of the sheep and cows since they were also used as storage containers for the spirit, just as the Bible says.

As Michael says, speaking as the Angel of the Lord, "I have gained glory in them," in the killing of the firstborn. "Glory" is spirit or spiritual wealth amassed. He gained spirit/glory through killing the firstborn of Egypt, because upon death of the vehicle the spirit returned to its source, which was God through Michael. Twice Michael says this. First he says it after the killing of the firstborns (human sons as well as sheep and cows) of Egypt, and then again, for the second time, when the Hebrews crossed the sea, and Egypt pursued them. They were killed as the sea closed off over them. The Angel of the Lord, Michael, said for the second time, "I gain glory again from all those."

THE NEW SOULS AND CIRCUMCISION

That spirit collected from Egypt, placed in Michael, was then placed together with the original spirit of the 144,000 Angels and 12 Archangels (himself) and combined. The individual fragments were then cut from the whole (or lump) and made into a new creation, a "soul." This new soul was created from the whole and placed into the bodies of the Hebrews through Moses at Mount Sinai. This was called circumcision, the true circumcision, also known as the placement of the soul in the heart center on the 8th day.

The first time there were individual souls/seeds, or fragments of the Creator's Spirit through Michael, was at Mount Sinai, and the term used for incarnation was "circumcision." This is the first time the Hebrew's were circumcised with the soul of YHVH, God of Israel and God of Gods, which came from all of the spiritual material recovered out of Egypt. All of the spiritual material of Israel and Michael (same, Michael is Israel) along with all spirit recovered from the Nephilim, was put together into one lump. Mount Sinai was the first time the Hebrews were circumcised (had the soul of YHVH placed with their bodies) and the first time that individual souls directly from the Creator's wealth (spirit) were placed into form.

THE TWO CIRCUMCISIONS

There are two circumcisions. One is the "seal," or "sign," of circumcision, which is the cutting of the foreskin. That marked the bodies that we were allowed to incarnate in, and they were all male. And there was "true circumcision," which Paul talks about later and YHVH speaks about in Jeremiah, which is circumcision in the heart by/of the Spirit. The seed, or soul, is placed into the heart center or attached to the heart center. YHVH talks about that, saying, "I will give you a new heart and a new spirit." The new spirit was his (not his through Lucifer) and placed into the heart center, not the mind, which was the ego. Yet the Spirit of Lucifer remained as the mental consciousness. Hence the term "double minded."

"SOULS" AND "LIVING SOULS"

These new souls were *not* "Living Souls," which are Nephesh Haya, which were Spirits or Angels or Gods. Adam, all the way through the 12 patriarchs (Archangels), sons of Yakov, and the 144,000 were all Living Souls. Living Souls were Angels, Spirits, or Gods, just as Christ called them in Psalm 82 – "Ye are Gods, all Sons of the Most High." Living Souls or Spirits incarnated first-born to first-born *only*. The new fragments, which are *souls* that are placed into form in order to refine the spirit, are not the same. Nephesh Haya (Living Souls) and Nephesh (souls) are two different things. Living Souls are Spirits, Angels and Gods. Souls are *fragments* or *aspects* of an Angel or Spirit or God. This new spiritual material (souls) was first placed into form at Mount Sinai in the bodies of the Hebrews. Yet they were direct fragments of the Creator since only the Hebrews carried the Spirit of YHVH.

INDIVIDUAL KARMA BEGINS

Individual karma (sin) was ordained to govern the refining process, which was through Israel. Israel was the Angels and the Hebrews were the flesh bodies. YHVH talked about this throughout the Old Testament. "I will refine you as silver, I will refine you as gold, and I will purge the dross from you." Israel was both the souls and the Spirits; the 144,000 and their fragments; the new material placed into the bodies of the Hebrews. That is what happened. As I stated above, the 144,000 Angels incarnated first-born son to first-born son. They were the Spirits, and the rest were souls placed into the second-born, the daughters, and all of the rest of the family other than the first-born. The children of the Hebrews became storehouses of the spirit grown from Israel, replacing the first-born sheep and cows which were the previous storehouses for the spirit.

SIN IS KARMA

Understand that sin is karma in the Old Testament. You were purged or cleansed from your sin (karma) by being put into the "fire," which is incarnation. Sin and trespass are the same thing.

As Paul speaks in Romans 3:20, "For by the law is the knowledge of sin..." The law is the giving of the soul and the beginning of the refining process.

The law is spiritual, as it says in Romans 7:12 & 13 – "The law is justification of the spirit through the flesh." This was the task of Israel.

Romans 5:13 – "For until the law, sin (karma) was in the world but sin was not imputed when there was no law."

There was karma, but it was not yet applied to the personal account until the justification, or refining program, began.

Isaiah 40:2 – "Speak tenderly to Jerusalem and proclaim to her that her hard service has been completed and that her sin has been paid for and that she has received double for all her sins."

Romans 2:5 – "But according to your hardness and unrepentant heart, treasure up unto yourself wrath. God, who will render every man according to his deeds (karma) tribulation and anguish upon every soul of man that does evil..."

Micah 7:13 – "The Earth (soil) will become desolate because of its inhabitants, the result of their deeds."

1 Peter 4:1 – "He that has suffered in the flesh has ceased from sin."

LUCIFER WAS THE ORIGINAL SIN

Sin applied to your account was karma. But basically when you look at sin from the New Testament, it is different. All were under sin because all carried the Spirit of Lucifer – that was the sin. That was the original sin that Christians talk about who do not understand spiritual things. They think the original sin was Adam disobeying God. No, it was the *outcome* of the disobedience that was the sin. The Spirit of Lucifer would be grown, not God directly. This was the sin. The sin was the Spirit incarnate, which we worked and grew. That is why all were under sin.

INDIVIDUAL KARMA BEGAN AT MOUNT SINAI

So here is the answer to the original question. The first time that karma began being applied directly to an individual soul, not a collective or group, was at Mount Sinai through the Hebrews. Understand that sin, or karma, governs the refining process. It began after we recovered the wealth or spirit that remained in Egypt that belonged to the Creator God. This was a long time coming, and it essentially ended the war in Heaven and on Earth. Although still, the remaining Nephilim would be dealt with as the Hebrews took possession of Canaan. Once again the killing of the first-born sons and the first-born sheep and cows was necessary to recover the spirit within.

Part one of the Creator's plan was to recover all of the spirit.

Part two of the Creator's plan was Israel, which was to refine the wealth recovered through the bodies of the Hebrews. Why refine it? In order to return it above the firmament to the Celestial realm. There are no flesh bodies above and there is no refinement or increase (growth) of spirit. All of this takes place in the 3D world only, through the flesh body. It is through the flesh body that refining and purifying take place. In growing, you are performing your service to the Creator, but first to yourself.

Remember, this entire world was set up to grow and refine the Spirit of God through the flesh body.

DOES THE KARMA WE CLEAR COME FROM THE LAST LIFE OR SEVERAL LIFETIMES?

That is a good question, but it is only applied if you are a soul in the 1 through 9 group. Remember, you are not clearing karma if you are a Master vibration. That is not your goal and not your purpose. If you are in the 1 through 9 cycle of incarnations, then you are subject to regular karma, and your soul's first purpose is to clear your karma. So if you are between 1 and 9, and not a walk-in, then your karma that you are clearing now came from your last lifetime.

Karma is earned in one lifetime and cleared in the next, unless you are a 9, as I explained earlier. If you are in your 9 incarnation, and it is the most difficult one, it takes many, many lifetimes to complete. That is because you are incurring and clearing karma in the current lifetime, while you are also clearing the karma earned during the previous lifetime. You must do this to be finished with your incarnations on this planet. This is the requirement for ascension, being karma free. You cannot enter the Celestial realm with darkness on your books. Being karma free also determines your vibration. Vibration = Ascension.

If you are in the karmic cycle, which is 1 through 9 on the incarnation wheel, you are clearing karma from your past life while you are incurring karma in this life, which you will work off in the next life.

IS IT POSSIBLE FOR SOMEONE TO BE KARMA FREE AND NOT KNOW IT?

No, and why is that? It is because karma governs your understanding, your spiritual awareness, and your rate of ascension. Karma governs the awareness. The more karma you work off, the more aware you become. When you get to the top you are aware that you have no karma. Even if the human hasn't figured it out yet, both the soul and the ego know that they are subject to instant karma.

Karma, or clearing of karma, determines awareness. When you get to the point where you have no karma, you know you have no karma, for two reasons. 1) You are aware enough to know, because karma has determined your awareness, and 2) bad things aren't happening to you anymore that you have no control over. Remember, karma really is darkness. Light is sent to balance that darkness. As that happens, you grow. As you grow you will get to the level where there is no more darkness generated. All that there is, is awareness. One is then aware that there is no more darkness.

Karma is the system which determines your ascension. It determines that you will grow, guarantees that you will grow. When you have grown, when you are an 11, 22, or 33, a Master vibration, if you have made that choice to continue, then you know that you have no karma, and this is what I am talking about. When you get to the top of the chart you know that you have no past karma, but then you will come to understand *instant* karma. The Scriptures speak to this also in Romans 1:19 – "Because that which may be known of God is manifest in man."

The amount of God within (spirit) determines the understanding of God. With each incarnation you grow in light or spirit. As this happens you become more of this light and are more aware of spiritual things.

THE EGO LEARNS THROUGH EXPERIENCE

You will figure it out. You will come to understand, "Wow I do this and something bad happens." After many incarnations we are not ignorant, and the ego is very, very tricky. It understands, believe me. The ego learns through direct experience. It actually gets crafty at creating karma. The ego tries all different kinds of ways to increase the darkness without suffering harm to its body. When there is a trespass, who is really paying the penalty? The physical body is where it is played out. The soul is passive and not subject to the physical consequences because it is attached to, not within, the body.

This is why the soul does not exist within the flesh body. It cannot be subject to the darkness that is incurred. Yet the soul is chained, or connected, to the heart center by the silver cord. The heart center is where the Mind of God exists, and is the only thing not controlled by the ego/mind.

EGO AND BODY SUFFER THE CONSEQUENCES

You, the body, are paying the price. When your body pays the price for karma, your ego pays it too, doesn't it? It does the time in prison with you. So this is what a lot of you do not understand, the ego creates the darkness but it also pays the price. It takes on the pain, and it feels what you the body feel.

As you get older (spiritually speaking) and with more incarnations, your egos get craftier at creating darkness without paying the physical toll. Your egos find new ways to increase evil and darkness, which is karma, so that they continue to ascend. And so you, the flesh body, do not have to pay such a high price, because the flesh is the one paying.

The ego and the body both suffer the consequences of your trespasses.

CONTRARY TO WHAT IS COMMONLY TAUGHT AND BELIEVED KARMA IS NOT A PUNISHMENT

There are so many different teachings about karma, and so many teachers saying all sorts of different things. And it creates a lot of misunderstandings among people. Some are led to believe that karma is a punishment, or that it directly creates blockages in relationships, as well as illness and other things. It is not a punishment and it does not do those things in the way most people think. Karma is not about punishment, nor is it about good and evil. Karma is about balance and growth. By maintaining balance, karma controls the growth of spirit in this world.

There is one system and it is karma, there is no other system. It is the Creator's system. It has specific rules. What is taught by the teachers out there is all the same thing mostly. Some may have some direct information, and hopefully it is from a high level, but mostly it comes from everything they have read, everything they have heard, and what is commonly taught. I teach something different, but my teaching comes direct. I present to you what God presents to me.

RELATIONSHIPS & SOUL GROUPS

Let's talk about how karma affects relationships. Karma is incurred and cleared between people. Relationships are where the most karma and clearing of karma is incurred, and we usually incarnate in soul groups. Every person you have been in contact with in this lifetime, or have had any type of relationship with, whether it's a friend, lover or enemy, you have incarnated with before.

You have all incarnated with your children before. Your husbands and boyfriends, you have all incarnated with each of them before. And the reason this is done is because of how karma works. Remember, it takes two to Tango. The Creator's system requires relationships to stimulate the necessary growth.

When any two come together, three things can happen. There is an exchange of light and light, light and darkness, or darkness and darkness. Each time it is cause and effect. Of the three types of energy exchange, light and dark, and dark and dark are the most common, and stimulate the most growth, spiritually speaking. Karma cannot be incurred or cleared without two people involved. Remember, karma is incurred for a trespass against another human being.

DIRECT AND RANDOM KARMA

There are two ways to incur one's karma. They are direct karma and random karma. For example, it is much easier to incarnate with your soul family or soul group because, for your karma earned in the last lifetime, most of it came from the trespasses against those you were incarnate with as part of your group during the past lifetime. The people you know, like your friends, family, and associates. That is where most of it comes from, and your clearing comes from the same people. So you trespass against them, and they in turn trespass against you. And you also clear karma through them. You incur and clear, incur and clear. You actually create and wash each other's karma. This is why you incarnate most often together as a soul group. The soul group remains together throughout the incarnation cycle. This is usually choice #2 in the lifetime choices that we mentioned in earlier chapters.

INCARNATING *WITHOUT* SOUL GROUP

Sometimes, however, you will incarnate and not be in the flesh at the same time with your soul group, and this does happen, as sometimes you may choose a life at a different time. The chosen lifetime could be 20, 40, 80, 120 years later, or longer, depending upon how you choose to clear your karma earned from the last incarnation. If those that the karma was incurred through are not incarnate with you, then you will be subject to random karma, which is a lot heavier and harder than direct karma. So then you may be subject, for example, to a car accident, or broken legs. Or you are subject to a broken heart or a lifetime of horrible relationships. This is the harder path to clearing karma. To be clear, random karma is random. You incur it randomly and you clear it randomly. It's like being thrown to the wolves.

INCARNATING *WITH* SOUL GROUP

But the easier path and the normal path is when you incarnate with your soul group and boom, boom, boom, it is directly worked off. They increase yours, and you increase theirs. You clear theirs, and they clear yours. Because, if you think about it, who can increase the drama around you more than your family and friends? This includes boyfriends and girlfriends. Comparatively, what about the neighbor, way down the block, maybe that you wave to once a month? Can he/she increase or deplete your karma? Not very easily. It would be pretty difficult.

Yes, random karma can work through anyone, yet the preferred method is group karma through incarnating together. One both gains and removes karma much easier through incarnating in the same groups, with the same souls, again and again, together.

PAIN, ILLNESS, AND AVOIDANCE OF KARMA

Realize that we want you to stay incarnate. We want you to work it off. In other words, *not* as a punishment or retribution. Your karma will not result in illness of the body. Anybody teaching you that, "oh you are sick because it is your karma," or "you have got cancer because it is your karma," does not understand. They are full of baloney.

Pain comes through avoidance of karma. Avoiding the balancing of great amounts of darkness (karma) leads to imbalance, which causes pain and eventually illness. The pain is the warning sign to stop the ego from its rampage. The normal workings of karma ensure that you will be illness free. The body is the temple of God. The body is sacred and holy. The misunderstandings of karma have led some of you to believe that karma is a punishment, yet in truth it is a gift of God for your good!

Pain will cause illness, and avoidance of karma will bring more pain. I think what has happened is that your teachers don't have the ability to explain the entire karmic process, so they are throwing out end results without taking you through the mechanics. I always take people through the mechanics. The Creator takes me through the mechanics so that I am able to explain step by step the how, why, and what.

Here's the mechanics.

Yes, illness can happen. Your karma is actually gained through the increased darkness. Karma is darkness which is increased by, and through, you. Let's say you, the ego, increase the darkness and then do everything possible to avoid making that change necessary to bring the light in. You increase the darkness, increase the darkness. Remember, as I mentioned in a previous chapter, as you are increasing darkness (gaining karma) life is at its best and good things are happening. It is when light is sent to balance that things become difficult for you. So the ego must make a decision when to stop. The ego does not always want to let the good times end.

PAIN FORCES THE RETURN

Eventually what happens from that, because you must always be in balance, is that pain comes. The pain forces you to return to the Creator and ask for the healing which is the light sent to balance. In the Old Testament, YHVH speaks to Israel saying, "When I slew you, you would seek me."

The Creator will do anything and everything to return you to him (balance light with dark). Now you are no longer killed, but you are subject to pain. The pain will cause the illness, but the illness is not from the karma. It is through the avoidance and increase of darkness without the balance of light. The return to God (the light) brings the healing and washing of your karma. That is the true use of free will.

The illness comes from the body being out of balance, not from karma. The Creator needs you to grow, not die. When your body is out of balance between dark and light, yes, you are subject to illness, and sometimes great illness. And with that comes the pain, causing you to change.

Living with the pain caused by unbalanced darkness or karma, leads to direct illness. But through pain comes change and light and, of course, growth.

The ego is very powerful, and darkness is the key to its ascension. Great pain is sometimes necessary, especially with younger egos, to get them to cease from the incurring of darkness.

IS THERE SUCH A THING AS
ANCESTRAL KARMA?

No, there is no ancestral karma, assuming you are asking if it comes from past family members who were *not* "you." But again, the answer is yes and no, because your karma technically is from your ancestors, because *they* were *you*. If you are an old soul and you walk-in (all old souls incarnate by walk-in, and also at that time through the first born) then, yes, basically your karma goes all the way back to that time. I am my own grandpa, so in that sense, yes.

But there is no leftover, or left behind, karma. You work on the current and previous lifetime. You do not go from a 5 to a 6 until all karma earned in the 5 is done. You do not go from a 6 to a 7 until all karma earned in the past lifetimes is cleared. One may incarnate in the 6 cycle three or four (or more) times until all karma incurred in the previous cycle is balanced.

SINGLE SPIRIT VS INDIVIDUAL SOULS

Let's say this. There was ancestral karma back when it was a single Spirit going from father to son and from son to son, because it was the same individual. It was the same Spirit. So that is why it carried its own karma through those various incarnations. The sons were responsible for the father's karma (sin) because it was the same Spirit. YHVH says, "I will hold the son responsible for the sins of the father."

But now that they are individual souls, the father is a different soul than the son, so it is a different situation. You are your own soul, fragmented from your own Angel above the firmament. Your Angel has no karma. You are not going to carry someone else's karma. You are either carrying your own or none at all.

But having said all that, you must know that the "you" before, in the last lifetime (and in all the previous lifetimes) is, spiritually speaking, your own ancestor, since you incarnate within your own genetic line. I could say that some of my past karma has come from my great-great-great-grandfather. Yet that is still "me."

CAN SOMEONE WHO IS NOT A MASTER NUMBER AND IS NOT A WALK-IN SERVE THE CREATOR?

The answer to this question depends on how it is meant. First of all, understand that in the general sense, everybody and everything in this physical world serves the Creator. It does not matter who you are, what you are, or what you believe. If you are an atheist who doesn't believe in God, you serve. If you are black, white, green, red, yellow, or blue, you serve. If you are Hindu, Buddhist, Muslim, or Christian...you may believe something totally different, but you still serve.

All who are incarnate serve, period. If you are in a human body, you serve the Creator. That is why you are here. You serve the Creator through serving and growing yourself. Everybody serves. There is no way around it. This is the service that all in a physical body perform. You grow the Creator by growing yourself. *What is caused in the flesh has its effect in the Spirit.* If you are in the flesh then you are growing the spirit. That is your main purpose and why you are here.

But if the question is asking about serving the Creator in the sense that you are going to directly serve as a son or a daughter (of God), or as a world karma server, then no. You cannot serve with karma. We talked about this in earlier chapters. Let's go over it again for clarity.

THE SOUL'S FIRST PURPOSE

The soul's first purpose is commanded by God, by the Creator who put you here. That first purpose is to clear karma. In doing that, it ensures that you will grow, and in doing so, you grow the Creator. This is your purpose and the purpose of all incarnate in the normal cycles between 1 and 9. To grow in light. To become and return (ascend).

MASTERS SERVE DIFFERENTLY

Master vibrations serve in a different manner. Understand that you are finished with your incarnations after completion of the 9 cycle. At this time you can return to the Celestial where you were first cut from, or you can continue your service by serving the Creator directly. In the latter instance you cannot have any karma, because the first purpose of the soul, commanded by the Creator, is to grow through clearing individual karma. This is in direct opposition to what you will be doing as a direct servant.

As a world karma server, as a son or daughter or direct servant of God, he may have you serving darkness. He may have you doing all kinds of strange things, both to benefit him and human kind. That will be in another book where we can elaborate more. But for now, just know that serving as a Master conflicts with your first purpose, which is to clear and balance your own karma. This is also by his command, yet it creates a conflict. One command conflicts with the other and that is why one command must be resolved before the other can be accepted.

So you cannot be a world karma server, you cannot serve

the Creator as a direct son or daughter, essentially as an Angel incarnate, if you have karma. You would be serving yourself first (having to balance personal karma) and not the Creator first. All Master vibrations are, or will be, world karma servers. As a Master vibration you are subject to instant karma. Why? Because when darkness is incurred you are sitting on the bench, so to speak. You are taken out of service until you are balanced. You cannot serve the Creator directly while you have karma on your books.

So, in summary, all serve. It is just *how* you serve that varies.

Let us go over it one more time for clarity. With karma on your account, you are serving yourself, because that karma must be cleared, or balanced, as a first priority. The end result is that everything serves God, and everything *is* God. There is nothing else but God. However, as a direct servant, you are serving God first and not yourself first, that is the difference. He/she must be the first priority. Like Christ says, you must love me before your son, your daughter, and everything else. That is how that works.

The Creator cannot be first as long as you have existing karma. You cannot serve humanity if you are required to serve yourself.

DID JESUS HAVE KARMA WHEN HE INCARNATED HERE ON EARTH?

No. Why would a Celestial entity, the Christ, have to work off karma? Why would he have any karma? No, he did not have karma. He came here as what? A direct servant of the Creator. You have to read 1 John, it tells you exactly what he came here to do, and he did not come to create Christianity. I will even give you the passage.

Most people read the Bible at the simple or homiletical level, which is far below what is necessary to understand the spiritual/mystical truth of God contained within it.

Here it is – 1 John 3:8 and 9 – "The Son of God was manifested that he might destroy the works (increase in spirit) of the devil. Whosoever is born of God does not commit sin, for his nature (God's Spirit) remains in him and there is no sin in him."

The sin they are referring to in that passage is the Spirit of Lucifer. All were under sin as the Bible states. Why? Because pre-Christ all carried the Spirit of Lucifer. In other words, the Spirit of God *through* Lucifer.

The bottom line is that he (Christ) came to destroy the works (spirit) of the "devil" or Spirit of the World (Lucifer). This was his first purpose. He came to put an end to, stop the increase (works) of, that Spirit. Christ was the Creator in form, as you will become (a son or daughter of God), once you have stood up to be counted and been accepted. Some of you already are and just are not aware.

Christ had no karma. The incarnation of the Christ Spirit in the flesh of Jesus had no karma.

THE ANCENSTRAL LINE TO JESUS

However, the line of Jesus, the line from Adam to Joseph, Jesus' flesh father, was subjected to karma. All who were incarnated in that line either grew or refined the spirit to get it to the point that it could be returned back to where it came from. Understand that the spirit had to be refined. The refining process is the law, justification (purifying) of the spirit through the flesh, which is the incurring and clearing of karma. That started at Mount Sinai when the Hebrews received the soul, a.k.a. circumcision.

Isaiah 28:28 – "Grain must be ground to make bread."

Grain (raw spirit) must be refined to make Holy Spirit. Raw spirit is turned into Holy or "purified" Spirit through refining in the flesh body.

So, yes, the Adamic line was subject to karma. However, Christ was born in the womb. He was made a life giving Spirit. He, himself, was not subject to karma, he was Christ. Mashiach. And therefore karma free.

As Scripture states, Christ is the Glory of Israel. He was the combination of all of their spirit/wealth previously refined and placed within him. It was passed down from Adam, from first born to first born to Christ, the sum of all of the glory/wealth/spirit grown through Israel, the 144,000 Angels. Christ and Lord Michael are one and the same.

Above the firmament in the Celestial they do not have karma. They do not need refining. There is no growth of spirit in the Celestial realm, except from what is grown down here and is sent above. Light exists there, darkness does not. We incarnate in order to experience darkness, the opposite polarity. We came here to experience evil, which does not exist in the realms where we come from.

So the answer is no. The Christ, incarnate as Jesus, did not have karma.

WHAT EXACTLY IS MEANT BY EATING THE BREAD AND DRINKING THE WINE?

This is not a karma question, but I love it anyway, because it is one of my favorite things to tell Christians. The really heavy one is – "You must eat my body and drink my blood" – that is the one that scares the heck out of everybody. Even Christ said that statement will drive many away. This question is basically the same thing, except the words are "bread" and "wine" instead of "body" and "blood."

First, I'll explain the metaphors. "Bread" is always "spirit." Specifically Holy Spirit or Christ's Spirit, the highest level of spirit. "Blood" is also used for Christ's Spirit and the Creator's Spirit. "Wine," throughout the O.T. and N.T., is always the metaphor for "soul."

There is an actual spiritual meaning behind this and I will explain it for you.

Blood is spirit (Holy Spirit) and wine is soul. So what Christ says is that, to enter into the Kingdom of God (the Celestial), you must eat my Spirit and drink my soul. "Eat" and "drink" are metaphors for "partaking of" or "sharing in;" to partake, as when Adam ate the fruit of Lucifer. Fruit is spirit or soul, wine is soul, and blood is spirit.

So what it really means is that you must eat (partake) of my body, which is the Kingdom of God. He is the head of the body, which is the Kingdom of God above the firmament, the Celestial realm. And you must drink of my blood (spirit). So you must share of (exist within) my body (the Kingdom) and share of my soul/spirit. That is what it means, which is exactly spiritually true; in other words, it is saying "become a member of the Celestial realm or kingdom by carrying my Spirit in you."

ALL NEW SOULS COME FROM CHRIST

All of the new fragments are cut from the risen Spirit of Christ Michael. Once again, share of the Kingdom of God = eat my body/bread. Drink my blood = partake of and grow my Spirit. Paul says the same thing in 1 Corinthians 12 in a different manner. "But in all these works that one and same Spirit, dividing to every man as he will." There is one source dividing to all. Christ Michael is that source from which all souls are divided, or fragmented, for the last 2,000 years.

It is the same thing as "eat my body and drink my blood," but with metaphors that are less direct you might say. The body is the Celestial realm (the Kingdom of God) and the blood is the Spirit. But here it is Spirit instead of soul. So it is share, or partake, of the Celestial realm, which is 5D, and share of, or partake, of his Spirit, which is the fragment or aspect that grows in all of those incarnated the last 2000 years or so, which are called "souls."

CARRIERS OF THE NEW FRAGMENT

Who are the direct people that he is talking to, those that will be taking on his new soul? Those are the Hebrews that he asked to entrust (to place in his possession) the glory/spirit which had been grown and refined since Mount

Sinai in and through their flesh bodies. They are going to move into the new Kingdom and get the new soul, which is essentially out of Lucifer and into Christ. They are surrendering the old spirit and receiving the new fragment of the Spirit from Christ Michael. It is called the Eternal Spirit or Holy Spirit. They were giving up their works (glory) for this.

What was grown/refined through the Angels of Israel was collected from the bodies of the Hebrews by Christ Michael, and it was returned above to the Celestial realm and then used to seed the new "holy soul" to all over the last 2,000 years.

1 Corinthians 12:11 – "That one and same Spirit (Christ) dividing to every man, individually, as he will."

DO OTHER PLANETS OR WORLDS HAVE KARMA?

There is one world created explicitly to grow the Creator, and that is this one. It is the only 3D world created for growing the spirit, and it is unique in this way. This entire world was created to grow the Creator through growing our selves.

We, as humans, are the only ones that have the soul fragment of the Creator. No other race/creation currently does. No E.T. group (beyond the firmament) nor any other form or creation has what we have. The E.T.'s participating here are from *within* the firmament, including Orion, Sirius, and the Pleiades. We, humanity, a.k.a. the creation created to grow the Creator, are composed of about 85% normal Earth-created (born) human life and 5% to 15% E.T. creations mixed in. Yet all have the same humanized form.

The E.T.'s were allowed to participate in this program, partly because we removed them and all other life forms before the firmament was put in place. We removed all of the Annunaki, and all of the Pleiadians, and every other aspect of life not human (or not originated from here) off of this planet. The wall/firmament now prevents anything, or any race, from tampering with the creation. There are no Annunaki coming back. What is the name of that planet that is supposed to come back every 5,000 years? Nibiru? There is no Nibiru coming.

The foreign life (E.T.) was allowed to participate here on Earth, at a small level, for three reasons. First, there was some regret for what we did to them (we the Angels). Second, they expressed desire as to the eternal life of the fragment consciousness, which only the humans would possess. And third, the potential for harassment of the creation existed, and by making them a part of the plan they could be an asset instead of a great liability. Remember, all serve God. All are created by God, including E.T.'s. He alone holds title of Creator.

The bottom line to the answer is no, there is no other 3D world in any universe which was set up explicitly to grow and extend the Spirit of God, through growing and extending the individual Spirits or souls. This world was built for that purpose and it is unique. Everything in this world is connected. One thing leads to another, the land to the crickets to the bugs to the food for the birds, to the chickens on your table. Everything was put here for man, the creation, to perform the ultimate task, which is growing the Creator through growing yourself.

EARTH IS THE CENTER OF THIS "WORLD"

This "world" has two parts to it. One is Heaven, also known as the "airy realms," which is Shamyim in Hebrew, for heaven or sky. And the other is Eretz in Hebrew, which refers to the solid ground (Earth) of the Kingdom of Heaven. The Kingdom of Heaven includes both the Earth (solid ground) and the Astral realm (sky or heaven), and is also known as "this world." The Kingdom of God is the Celestial above the firmament. The Celestial realm is another name for the Christ or Angelic realms.

The solid ground (our planet) is the center of the Creator's world. The Earth, not the Sun, is the center of this world and that is why the firmament is completely around the Earth. There is no other 3D world which grows the Creator like this one.

This is a test tube world set up as an experiment, a confined environment, to grow and awaken different parts of the Creator, through awakening yourself. Again, the Creator awakens or grows himself by placing himself into form. As the pieces (fragments) of him grow within this form, he is also grown. You, the body, are that form. You, the soul, are the fragment, or seed, that grows. You, the ego, also grow.

THIS IS THE ONLY WORLD THAT MATTERS NOW

Keep in mind, even though there are other worlds, this is the one that we are dealing with right now. This world is all that matters. This is the one that we are in, and until you get beyond this one why worry about others? Your work is here. Your existence is here. And what you do here will determine your next placement, so to speak.

The first step toward your lofty goal was set in motion the minute you incarnated into this world. The second step will be when you leave this world and return to the Celestial, when Lucifer hands you off to Christ in a perfected state of light.

There is nothing like this world, nothing compares to it. No other world or universe compares to this world that is under the firmament. And just so you know, yes, there are other worlds. Many in fact, but none of them have anything to do with you. You came here and you chose to come here, so none of that affects anything. That is why there is a wall around it, so nothing can effect the creation. That creation is *you*.

You chose to enter this adversarial world to experience evil, the polarity which does not exist where you/we come from. Darkness and evil are the fertilizer that grow light. There is no fertilizer (darkness/evil) in other realms that stimulates the growth of the creation.

WHY DO MASTERS STILL HAVE A VEIL IF THEY ARE NOT HERE TO WORK OFF KARMA?

The veil varies from soul to soul. The more light achieved, the more the veil is peeled away, like peeling an onion. The veil is the ego, or mind, that you think through. As I mentioned earlier, this is why you know if you have karma or not. The veil is diminished as one increases in light.

Do you think the worst thing you are veiled to is your past karma, so you cannot get around it? No, the worst things you are veiled to are how you died in your past lifetimes, and how evil some of you were in your past lifetimes.

What if you were unveiled and you knew everything? The Angels that were Israel were unveiled, and look what happened there. They were constantly offered (and sometimes accepted) deals, better than their deal with Michael, from other Gods, and suffered the wrath of YHVH.

Let us say that you were alive during the Spanish Inquisition and they cut off your toes, they put hot pokers up your rear, and they cut off your breasts one by one, which is all of the stuff that they did do! How would you like to be unveiled to that and relive it time after time after time?

Remember how the ego works. It uses the past to affect the present. How would you like to know that you were molested as a young boy in Greece 2000 years ago, over and over and over? Do I need to continue? The ego uses past memories to enforce itself upon you, to create action. Past memories are the source of the ego's greatest power over you.

WOULD YOU STILL PLAY THE GAME?

I think you all understand what you are veiled to. So there is more being veiled than just karma, a lot worse things. Not only that, not just the pain and the memories, but it is also this: how would you play the game if you weren't veiled? You would try to cheat the game, and you wouldn't play the game, if you knew all of the ins and outs. Or you just wouldn't care about it. You wouldn't even want to be alive, personally, and you would be terrified. If you knew that you were a child abuser, and you thought that you would in turn be abused somehow in this life for that, would you be terrified every minute of every day? Knowing that it was coming? I know I would.

If you weren't veiled through the ego, you would understand that you are not the body, not the human being. You would understand that the ego forces you to believe that. And you might just realize that you are a prisoner of the system. The veil keeps order among workers.

THERE ARE DIFFERENT LEVELS OF VEIL

The farther along the path you are, the more light that you carry. There are different levels of veil. Spiritually speaking, the greater the understanding, the less the veil. Remember, a 33 Master vibration doesn't mean that the vehicle (body) is any better (although it can and does carry more darkness and therefore more light). The basic difference between a

33 and an 11 is that they can carry more light. More light means more God, which means more understanding. Again back to Romans 1:19 – "What can be understood of God is manifest in man." The more Spirit that is in me, the more I understand spiritual things. The more God in me, the more I understand God.

So, yes, the higher the awareness and the more incarnations you've had, the more the understanding and the thinner the veil. Both ego and soul grow together. Believe me, there are lifetimes that I am not proud of. I have never known any where I have done any atrocious crimes. None that I can recall anyway. Yet, in the service of the Creator and in his name, there is much that humanity would call "evil" that I have done.

DO MANTRA OR FORGIVENESS
PRACTICES HELP?

There is no mantra, no forgiveness exercise, and no prayer that will take away your karma. Personal karma must be worked off (balanced) personally. This is how you grow. Now, if in your heart you turn to God, and ask him to help you, and genuinely express it, yes he will save you and send the light. But that is what he does anyway.

As we have said, karma is darkness. Darkness cannot be removed. It is placed in the flesh body where it must be transformed, changed, balanced by light. Darkness is still spirit, still God. Who can take God away?

Remember, you are your own savior! Karma the instrument to get you to return to God (ascend), to increase God through the increase of you by balancing and overcoming darkness. So no, a prayer is not going to do it. There are no shortcuts. You incur your karma and you remove your karma. This is how you bring God's Presence into being. Darkness stimulates light.

Anybody who teaches you that prayers remove karma should be sent back to spiritual elementary school. Interfering with one's karma is interfering with one's ascension. To remove karma from one (if it were possible) is to remove what is required to grow spiritually. Karma is not random, in the sense that *you* incur it and only *you* can decrease it. Through this Divine system you grow, spiritually speaking. If someone could remove your karma, they would be stunting or preventing your growth. It's not like removing a tumor or ridding you of a disease.

The point is, darkness is the key to your spiritual growth. Karma is the acquiring of darkness, which is the key to get you to turn to the light. Back to the scriptures again, as Michael/YHVH said to Israel, "When I slew you, you would seek me." He killed us to get us to return to him. No longer is that necessary. Through pain comes growth.

Our incarnations were filled with disasters when we turned from Michael and his loving embrace. We were as sheep to the slaughter. Turning from him was turning from our source. When we did, that source was no longer available to us. That no longer happens to those incarnate now. In other words, the more darkness created through evil, the greater the light required to balance or transmute it. It took a whole lot of pain, anguish, and suffering to get us, the Angels of Israel, to turn back to him. In the end, we realized that he (Michael/YHVH) was the source of our pain *and* our salvation.

IT IS ABOUT BALANCE NOT FORGIVENESS

So no, God doesn't allow you to praise him and say a mantra to get forgiveness of karma. It's not about forgiveness anyway, it's about balance. Through darkness you increase light. If a prayer were given that would decrease your karma (darkness), it would also decrease your light. Do you understand that? You are measured light equal to the darkness, so that would be an avoidance of karma, and God would be violating his own systems that he put into effect. God would be stunting his own growth. *God is all there is.* We all serve the one through serving ourselves. It is a joint purpose.

YOU ARE ASKING YOURSELF ANYWAY

Who are you asking to clear karma anyway? You're asking yourself, ultimately. All you are doing is asking yourself, because there is no God over karma. There is no Lord over karma. There is no Archangel over karma. Karma is self-manifested, self-disciplined, and self-dispensed. So nobody can remove or clear your karma but you. If anyone could, it would be a great trespass for that individual to clear your earned karma, and that trespass would be against the Creator himself! It would be like removing your Godliness. You are the God over your own karma. Remember, in increasing darkness you are still increasing God.

In summary, understand this: To remove or interfere with someone's karma is to interfere with one's ascension or spiritual growth.

And keep in mind, by saying that you would be asking your "self", we are not talking about the human self, but the "all of you." "You," as the human personality, are not conscious of the whole process. Not until now anyway. But you should be. You need to be. That is what I am trying to get you conscious of. That is why we are doing this. You should pray for understanding.

There are only two prayers I recommend: The Great Invocation and the Prayer of St. Francis. These are the two greatest prayers given to mankind.

The Great Invocation

From the point of Light within the Mind of God
Let Light stream forth into the minds of men.
Let Light descend on Earth.
From the point of Love within the Heart of God
Let Love stream forth into the hearts of men.
May Christ return to Earth.
From the center where the Will of God is known
Let purpose guide the little wills of men
The purpose which the Masters know and serve.
From the center which we call the race of men
Let the Plan of Love and Light work out
And may it seal the door where evil dwells.
Let Light and Love and Power restore the Plan on Earth.

The Prayer of St. Francis

Lord, make me the instrument of your peace.
Where there is hatred, let me sow love;
Where there is injury, pardon;
Where there is doubt, faith;
Where there is despair, hope;
Where there is darkness, light;
And where there is sadness, joy.

O Divine Master, grant that I may not so much seek
To be consoled as to console;
To be understood as to understand;
To be loved as to love.
For it is in giving that we receive;
It is in forgiving that we are forgiven;
And it is in dying that we are born to eternal life. Amen

DO ANGELS AND ARCHANGELS AND GODS AND LORDS HAVE KARMA?

No. Karma is and works in this world only; the 3D world under the firmament. It is God's program. Nothing above has karma because they are not subject to the polarities, as there is only light. They do not exist within a physical body (flesh) and they have no ego to serve as the catalyst to actuate karma. They are only light, and they only increase in, and through, light.

There is no need for them to increase the darkness to grow, because light is sent to them above from this 3D world. The evil/darkness required to grow light does not exist in the Celestial realms above.

Understand this, darkness is cause, and light is effect. Ego is cause, and soul is effect. The light grown through darkness here on this planet is what increases the upper Celestial realm. What you provide from here grows the entire creation and all worlds. For a moment, just imagine if you will that, through your service, all worlds are transformed. It is huge indeed.

What is caused by the ego has its effect where? On the soul, and thereby on the Spirit. The Creator's system is a downward manifestation of cause and effect. That is why you, the seed or soul, are planted in the flesh (soil). He, the Creator, makes changes to himself through himself (your flesh), because he is all in all, and you are in him. *What is caused in the flesh has its effect in the spirit* – both the soul here and your Angel/Spirit above the firmament, which are directly connected to each other.

Isaiah 37:31 – "Once more a remnant of the house of Judah will take root below and bear fruit (glory/spirit) above."

You create yourself above through the flesh below. This is why you came here. This is what this entire 3D world is, and was, created for; to build your realm above through the flesh body below. You continually balance darkness with light in the flesh body, increasing the mixture each time you are incarnate.

DO THEY HAVE A SIMILAR LAW TO KARMA ABOVE THE FIRMAMENT?

This is a good question. Once again, there is no law of karma. Karma is not a law. It is a Divine system which governs the entire creation of God in this 3D world. There is no law of karma, please do not use that term. Karma is a Divine system that controls an individual's ascension. It is part of the greater system itself, part of reality itself. There are laws *within* the system of karma that make up karma, but karma itself is not a law. It is larger than that. And more importantly, it is totally self-supported and administered by you, as I keep saying. Karma, like everything in this created world, is cause and effect based, but it is *not* a law.

Do they have karma up above? No, there is no karma above. Why would there be? It is not necessary. The creation above is grown through this world. The creation above is perfected. Its needs are not the same. It needs only light. It is grown only through light. All of the darkness and all of the evil is here in this world. The firmament ensures that darkness and evil do not spill over into the Celestial realms. The light grown out of the darkness in this world is carried above. Yes, I know, that raises another question. Let us talk about it.

THERE IS ONLY LIGHT ABOVE

Firstly, nothing above in the Celestial (or 5D) is evil. There is no darkness, only light, and there is one polarity, Michael.

Where is the opposite polarity? Down here. There is no opposite polarity above the firmament, so there is no darkness or evil there either. There is also no matter (not the kind we are familiar with anyway) to place the seed into to grow.

Does your Angel grow from darkness? No, the seed (you) grows through darkness or evil, as it is balanced by light. Everything above is light or light based. What is fed to the upper realms is light.

There is no opposite polarity in the Celestial because there is no need (nor method) to grow darkness in the Celestial realm. There is no darkness in the Celestial realm, so there is no karma and no growth above through the darkness. Darkness, evil, and negativity exist only in the 3D realm as the catalyst to stimulate light.

That is another purpose of the firmament, to contain the darkness in the 3D and 4D realms. The main reason you came here is to experience evil, which does not exist in the Celestial realm.

LIGHT EXISTS ABOVE BUT IS GROWN BELOW

Just to clarify, 5D or Celestial = Christ and Angelic realm. You have to realize that without an ego, without the negativity, and without the polarities, we are all one. It is the ego that enforces the illusion that we are separate from the Creator. It does this by establishing the false personality. There is no division and no growth of its own in the Celestial realm. The growth comes through *this* realm. That is why you came here, *to create yourself above through the flesh below.* That is why your Angel, God, or Elohim has placed itself (you) into the soil (body), to increase, to become, and to feed your Angel above. What does it eat? Light! Light *exists* above, but is *grown* below through darkness. The 3D realm is cause and effect based. What is caused in the flesh has its effect in the Spirit (Angel). The "you" that is here grows the "you" that is there, but it is done through the growth of yourself (soul and ego) here.

YOU ARE THE WORKERS AND THE GROWERS

The system above is not based upon growing light through darkness. It is based upon increasing light, period. They are the suppliers of light to offset the darkness that we generate here, and they are also the receivers of the light we send back. They above are becoming larger and larger Angels in order to become Archangels. Archangels become Lords, Lords become Gods (or Logos) of the Universes, and this is the ascension process. All of this is achieved through the supply of light, or spirit, generated from this world. You are the suppliers, the workers, the growers. Karma is the system that ensures that all will grow and supply light, or spirit, to the upper realms. And it is a perfect system.

You are just at the very beginning of the ascension process. I have incarnated close to 4 billion years and I am still at the beginning of it. Understand that the process above is not subject to the creation growing through evil. There is no evil or darkness, only light, in the Celestial realm.

You are the providers of light, and only you, incarnate, can provide this most precious commodity! Your pain here is their gain in there, in the Celestial realm.

COULD A SOUL REFUSE TO TAKE ON KARMA?

Yes and no. It's not that you can refuse karma itself, but you can refuse a particular incarnation. Existing karma is not a choice, it is a fact. But each incarnation is a choice to some extent.

You have (or are given) a limited number of choices as to which incarnation to take, and this choice is mostly about how fast you are going to work off your previous karma. As you, the soul, are in control of the lifetimes that you select to incarnate within, you have the options to determine your own rate of ascension. Christ, the first to return or ascend, took 76 lifetimes from Adam to Jesus. If you count them, it is 76.

We have already explained this earlier in the book. I cannot give you an exact number of choices of lifetimes that you may have, however it goes like this. You are shown one. If you say no, you are shown a second. With another no, you are shown a third. I don't know anyone that has gone more than three choices, and I know a lot of souls. By choice four or so, you are most likely into the "Goo." This is because, to your Angel, you are not growing it, and therefore not growing the Creator either. You are not feeding it, and you are a wasted seed that will not mature. To refuse incarnation, or to put off incarnation, is not acceptable.

Understand that the faster path is first offered whereby you might possibly balance all karma in that one particular incarnation. However, this would be the most difficult incarnation, with many obstacles to overcome. The second option might take three lifetimes, but it is a much easier path, with fewer (or easier) obstacles in the path.

So, as I said, you ultimately govern your own ascension as you choose the path by choosing the incarnation. The optimal path is to incarnate with your soul group. This is usually choice number two.

FREE WILL TO CHOOSE THE INCARNATION

You, the soul, do have free will in regard to incarnation choice. The *soul* possesses this free will. The ego is *not* involved in the choice to incarnate. So they will not just throw you into a body. But again, you will go back into the Goo if you do not choose to incarnate to clear your karma earned. As I mentioned above, I cannot give you an exact number of incarnations before you will pay this penalty, but if you are not growing your Angel by growing yourself it is counterproductive to why you came here.

I know I have always jumped at the first shot, and most of the older souls incarnate that I know have jumped at the first shot too. We just take the hardest lifetime. But there are those that don't. From my duties as a teacher above, I assist many incarnate in this realm, and three choices is pretty much the maximum number offered. But the second choice is the optimal one for incarnating with your soul group, and those who don't take the first will usually take the second.

Back to the original question, if you refuse to take on your karma, you are also refusing to incarnate. You can't incarnate and not take on your karma, assuming you have existing karma. And all 1-9 souls have karma, if they have previously incarnated. You, as a 1-9 soul, exist in the Astral realm, waiting to reincarnate. You are a fragment of a greater being above the firmament in the Celestial. So if the fragment does not incarnate, you might as well throw it back into the Goo and at least salvage something.

To refuse to incarnate is to refuse to grow. You *chose* to come here to grow. I don't know any instance when it has ever happened that a soul completely refused to incarnate. We *want* to grow. We want to become. It is "standing room only" above, trying to get into bodies. Everyone wants to be here. Growing is our destiny and only purpose. It is why we came here.

This is the only realm where the little seed can become a great tree.

WHY DOES THE SOUL CHOOSE
THE INCARNATION?

I have explained that while you are in the Astral realm between incarnations you will be given the options for the next lifetimes that are available to you. There are usually three options for incarnation as I have explained.

THE THREE OPTIONS

The first option is the fast track or hardest path, whereby you balance in the current lifetime all karma incurred from the past lifetime.

The second option, which is the most popular choice, involves incarnating with your soul group. In this option you will be incurring and balancing karma with those that you have done so for most of your incarnations. By choosing this option it could take several lifetimes to balance the karma from one previous lifetime. This is the safest choice and the majority of souls choose this option.

And finally, there is the third option, or slow road, whereby it could take many lifetimes to balance the incurred karma. After that you are pretty much out of options.

YOU WOULD THINK THE EGO CHOOSES

As the ego is active, and the driving force in your ascension, one might *think* that it would be the selector of the incarnation. After all, it controls every other aspect of incarnation, and every choice made while incarnate. But this would be untrue.

It is all about *balance*. Understand that God does not care about good and evil, as he is all things. This world functions through balance and imbalance. It's all about the balance between light and dark, right and left, spirit and matter. One offsets the other, assuring that we will grow, and thereby also the Creator.

As we have explained throughout this book, the ego grows and ascends through darkness. Its purpose is to bring darkness into form and it controls the amount of darkness that is created. The soul must bring light into the body in an equal amount to match that darkness.

THE EGO WOULD ALWAYS CHOOSE THE HARDEST PATH

The ego's purpose is to ascend through darkness, and it is increased, or made larger, through darkness, not light. Thus said, would the ego not want to do this as soon as possible?

The ego would always choose the hardest incarnation, bringing in the most darkness that it could in order to ascend in the quickest time.

This is an automatic choice. You, the creature, may feel that darkness is "bad," but to your ego it is food, bliss, and all that it seeks! Now you, the soul, must bring light from above to match the measure of darkness that you, the ego, create.

As a younger soul, using a 5 level as an example, it is not able to bring unlimited amounts of light from above to offset all of the darkness that the 5 level ego can generate. Understand that here in the 3D world darkness *is*, but light comes from one source above the firmament. There is no limit to the darkness that the ego can generate, if allowed. But the light that can be brought to the body through the soul is limited to the age and size of the soul. All things being equal, the 5 ego can generate more darkness than a 5 soul can offset with light.

In order to maintain balance, the soul holds power over the choice to incarnate by selecting the incarnation based upon its ability to bring light to the darkness generated by the ego. The soul almost always chooses the safe path which is number two. Both the soul and its Angel choose the life path or incarnation.

There are souls that do take option one. Masters (older souls) do it all the time, since they have been incarnate enough times to know what happens and what is required to maintain balance.

What happens if the soul cannot balance the amount of darkness generated by the ego? Can you say "walk-in"?

Thus said, hopefully you can see why the life path decision is made by the soul, rather than the ego.

IS THE AMOUNT OF KARMA DISPENSED BASED ON THE SOUL'S ABILITY TO OVERCOME?

Karma is not dispensed. There is no dispenser of karma other than you. Karma is darkness applied to your account. It is darkness which you have created for yourself through your choices. Darkness must always be balanced with light.

You are no more evil or dark than you are great in light, so there is no amount of karma that you could have earned that isn't always balanced. That is why it says in the Bible, and it is also spiritual law, "Nothing bad can happen to you that you are not prepared to deal with," because your darkness is never greater than your light. If it is, it is only momentarily until it is balanced, if you understand what I am saying. You are the cause of your own darkness.

Once again there is no one person, no God, and no Angel that hands out, or dispenses, your karma. It is you. You are the one that earned it, and you are the one that works it off.

God's business is what?

Spirit.

You are an independent contractor. A 1099 employee (this is the tax form in the USA for independent contractors) that takes the material/product/spirit from God, and you grow it to make it larger. How do you do this? It's automatic. You grow it through incurring karma and then balancing that karma that you have incurred; by bringing light to darkness. Just as Scripture states in Romans 12 – "The Spirit is given for profit." Your purpose is to grow it, to turn a "profit" from the amount you were originally given.

At your highest form you are the Spirit. As a fragment (soul) you are growing yourself, and thereby growing your Angel/Spirit above the firmament, the rest of you. You are also growing the Archangel, which in turn grows the Christ, and when everything is merged, will make the primary Spirit larger, which is Michael and God the Creator.

So that is the purpose, and that is the point. You are a seed, a fragment of your Spirit above the firmament in the Celestial realm. You are not yet a Spirit. You are a fragment of your Spirit, which is called a soul. Your Spirit is the same as your Divine Self, Solar Angel, or I Am Presence. It fragments itself and places a smaller piece of itself (like a seed) into the soil, to grow. You are that seed, and the flesh body is the soil.

The ego creates the darkness that the soul overcomes by bringing light to balance that darkness. As the ego and soul are always in balance (in power, spiritually speaking), the ego cannot bring more darkness than the soul can overcome. Remember, the soul has chosen the lifetime to ensure this. Just as Michael and Lucifer are equally balanced in power, neither of them having an advantage, likewise the fragments (egos and souls) are also equal in power.

DOES KARMA INVOLVE PREDETERMINED EXPERIENCES IN THE CURRENT LIFE FOR THE 1-9 SOULS?

No, nothing is predetermined. Anybody who tells you it is predetermined doesn't understand or has received false information. That is New Age fiction. There is nothing predetermined. The Creator's system is cause and effect. In this world everything is cause and effect based. Just once more for those blocked to this understanding. Everything in this world is based upon cause and effect. Without the cause there is no effect. Thus said, can anything possibly be pre-determined?

Here is the only thing predetermined: The Creator will grow. Why? Because he is all there is. There is no adversary. There is nothing to thwart his purpose. He is all the pieces in the puzzle, the dark and the light, the good and the bad. If the cause is random then the effect is also. If you have any kind of free will, then the cause and the effect from that cause are based upon your choices. And, as that is true, the only thing predetermined is that, through all of this, the Creator wins! As no matter what choice you make, bad or good, he always gains. You could also say that light is predetermined.

A GAME OF CHESS AGAINST YOURSELF

Let me give you an example. If you are playing a game of chess and you are playing against yourself, first you move the white pieces, and then you turn the board and move the black pieces. There can be only one outcome because there is only one player. God the Creator always wins. Even if there is a tie, the one who plays both sides still wins both sides because he *is* both sides. With each movement of a piece in the game (you), whether forward or backward (good or evil, light or dark), there is gain for the one who owns the whole game.

The final outcome, the victor of the game, may not have been decided yet on this go around. But as the game is played, and each piece (you) is moved, there is gain. The gain posts regardless of whether it is to the dark side or to the light side. Regardless of whether a white piece is moved or a black piece is moved, the game proceeds forward.

THERE IS ONE PLAYER AND ONE WINNER

The back and forth is what creates the dynamics, and thus only one result is guaranteed. There is one player and one winner. From your point of view you see darkness as bad and light as good, but I am telling you that is not God's view. It is not how God sees. As he has said, he is all things. No matter what choice is made, darkness or light, God grows.

Back to karma, there are different levels of trespass and hence different levels of karma, and these come through choices. Darkness is measured based upon the size and type of the trespass, and then an equal amount of light must be sent (or brought) to offset the darkness (trespass). Also, it goes back to soul groups. We normally incarnate together, so there are no random acts of having to work off karma, at least not in the majority of incarnations.

As the majority of one's karma is gained and cleared through souls groups, the quickest and easiest for all parties involved is to work off karma through those that you have incurred it from. You gain from them, and they gain from you. Since you are incarnate together at the same time, you are always in some kind of relationship together as family or friends or even coworkers. Thus said, you are consistently incurring and balancing between yourselves and there is no need for the ego/soul to seek and create random acts against others.

YOU HAVE BEEN ALL THINGS

There is no predetermined experience that you need to go through. Understand that the system insures that you have been all things. You have been white, and you have been black. You have been abused, and you have been the abuser. You have been murdered, and you have been a murderer. Do you understand what I am saying? Inevitably, karma ensures that you have created and done all acts, and had all acts created and done to you.

What I am giving you here is an example to help you understand that you have been all things and done all things. But karma is no longer an eye for an eye, since Christ. It is equal measures of light to darkness. However, if you choose the first path (the primary incarnation, the fast track to ascension as I have explained above) then yes, eye for an eye karma becomes a distinct possibility, since you are balancing all of it in one lifetime rather than over 3 or 4 lifetimes.

When you have reincarnated for a long, long time, and are

incarnate now as a Master vibration, you have been all things, male and female, rapist and raped. You have been and done everything, but there is nothing predetermined, except as I explained above (God always wins).

This world was created for the sole purpose of growing the Creator through growing the smaller pieces of him that he places into form (you). Thus said, the predetermination is what? God will grow himself through himself. The pieces (you) are doing the growing. It really is that simple.

THE PLAN IS SIMPLE

The Creator is simple. His plan for you (himself) is simple. I understand your egos (minds) want to make it more complicated. You want to make it a great mystery that no one can know. And it was! But no longer. We, above, have worked very hard to reduce the truth to simple words that anyone can understand. No metaphors. No big words that you must be a scientist to understand. No new parables to unravel. Perhaps it is the simplicity of my words that your ego/mind will reject?

I do not like to quote other people, however I present this one because I teach the same thing. I feel that this quote very clearly states the truth of humanity's condition.

"Sometimes people hold a core belief that is very strong. When they are presented with evidence that works against that belief, the new evidence cannot be accepted. It would create a feeling that is extremely uncomfortable, called cognitive dissonance. And because it is so important to protect the core belief, they will rationalize, ignore, and

even deny anything that doesn't fit in with the core belief." –
Frantz Fanon

We recommend that you read the above quote several times until you realize the truth of it.

The truth of the Creator is not complicated. It's very simple. God is all there is. He places himself (you) within himself (your body) to increase himself (the Whole) by increasing you (the parts). We are all the same, and yet we are also each unique. Each fragment is at its own level of spirit (light) within, affected by unique choices made here on the way back to the Celestial.

WE ARE THE CREATOR'S BODY

We all are the matter which makes up what you could call the Creator's body. There are planets and stars and galaxies and universes, and all vary in countenance (brightness). There is no duality, there never was nor could there ever be. How can there be? If there is only one, which there is, then he/she is all things. All matter, seen and unseen, formed and formless. Nothing is separate from the "One." Thus it can be said that we are all "of" God.

Those who say that we must dissolve the duality that separates us from the Creator or "oneness" do not understand the truth. There is no duality. There is no separation between you and the Creator. You are in him and he is in you. Every aspect of you is made of him. The flesh body is him. The Astral body is him. The Light Body or Angelic Self is also him. Is this world separate from him? Where is the duality?

I am not a scientist. However, I am pretty sure of this. Science will verify that all matter in this universe contains the same elements, and is ultimately the same "stuff" at the most fundamental level. Why? Because it all comes from the same source and *is* the same source.

Spirit and matter are one and the same. All matter, whether seen or unseen, is energy or spirit vibrating at a different rate. All matter comes from, and is, one source. No matter what you call it, it is all ultimately the same stuff. Divine stuff. God stuff. And all matter is consciousness in various states of transformation.

Matter is energy (spirit or light) waiting to transform. This is what you can see and touch. Spirit (energy or light) is matter transformed. This is all that you cannot see or touch. The Creator is all of this.

We've said it many times, but *the Creator is all there is.* There is no separation from himself. The only duality or separation is conceived in, and through, the ego. The only illusion that "is" is that you are convinced that "you" are this flesh body and therefore separate from the Creator.

Here is a verse from the scriptures about duality:
Ephesians 4:6 – "One God and Father of all (Creator) who is above all, and through all, and in you all."

The verse above should be crystal clear. The terms "through all" and "in you all" leave no room for misunderstanding. There is no duality. It is an illusion and not true.

HOW FAST IS INSTANT KARMA?

We talked about it earlier, but it's a good question and we will continue with it.

As a Master vibration subject to instant karma, you have decided to reincarnate to serve humanity and no longer yourself. There is a different purpose and a different set of rules. The biggest change in the rules, so to speak, is in the way you are subject to karma. No longer do you incur karma in the past lifetime and then balance it in the current lifetime. As a Master, you earn and clear karma within the same lifetime, and you are required to balance said karma "instantly."

The amount of time you will take to clear this karma depends upon how important you are to the Creator. Does the Creator play favorites? Yes he does! I am telling you he does, but the written proof is in the Scriptures, including the Gnostic Gospels and various other Apocrypha, etc.

The parable of the workers of the Kingdom of Heaven (this world) in Matthew 25:14 is quite clear. It explains how Christ Michael rewarded the servants/workers that returned a profit on the Lord's goods (spirit). One did very well and was rewarded greatly. Another did pretty well and was rewarded, but less so. One did nothing and was actually punished. What he had (spirit) was taken and given to another who had already shown success. Like an employee in a large company, those who produce more usually get paid more and are more respected and revered by their "boss."

Remember, you must be in balance to serve the Creator in a direct manner. As a Master vibration who has volunteered to return to this world, to serve the Creator and humanity rather than yourself (this is a high level of service), you cannot be imbalanced for even a short time and continue to serve him. If you are a world karma server and taking on darkness or light (and you may not even know you are doing this), you cannot be imbalanced, because that immediately takes you away from being that world karma server and changes the focus to your own personal karma.

So time is of the essence you might say. When you committed to serve the Creator directly, agreements were made. One of those was that, through no acts of your own, your karma earned would be washed by a higher source. You have nothing to do with it, it is automatic. It happens automatically and you have no ability to change it through so-called free will.

YOU ARE THE CREATOR'S GREATEST TOOL

When you committed to serve humanity and the Creator, any free will that you might have had was taken away. Those of you who are Master vibrations know this. "Of thy own self, thou can do nothing." The purposes are aligned, the Creator's and yours. You are the greatest "tool" in the Creator's tool box. You are the hammer, and no weapon of man forged against you may stand.

For those that are subject to instant karma (11, 22, 33, and walk-ins), for the time period that you are imbalanced with karma, you are an ineffective servant. You are sitting on the bench, so to speak. The game is playing and you are not batting. You are in the tool box, but not in use. This is why you have instant karma; to return you to the service of the Creator as soon as possible, by balancing your karma quickly or instantly. And you don't need to do anything. It is all out of your hands.

It could be minutes, it could be seconds. I have heard some people taking two days to balance, but most people get it within the same day, in minutes or hours. With me it is instant. My karma is instant.

You have agreed for it to be this way. You are an ineffective tool when you have karma. Instant karma puts you back into the game very quickly.

Also understand that as a Master vibration you have incarnated enough times that you rarely incur great amounts of darkness or karma. You are quite aware of how karma is incurred and what happens when you do. Usually the trespasses are slight and of the mental kind. Thus said, the penalty or effect of the cause (trespass) is also minor. In many cases the effect could be a stubbed toe, or locked keys in your car, or having to chase your dog that got out of the house. These are just a few examples of the types of instant karma you can get. I am always subject to the strangest types of instant karma.

THE SPILLED SOUP

Here is a funny story. During a recent radio show that we

were doing, I had just been brought some hot soup. Every once in a while I try to eat a little during the two-hour show. I made a comment in jest that was out of context about a listener that I thought was funny. It was a mental trespass, no doubt. In fact, I believe one listener said, "He's gonna get karma for that." Still laughing at my comments and the listener saying I would get karma for that, I picked up my soup, went to grab the spoon to take a mouthful, and somehow the spoon flew out of my hand, and the hot soup went into my lap. All of this happened while I was live on the radio. Coincidence? No. I knew, just as all the listeners knew; that it was the equalizer, my instant karma. I have experienced instant karma for so many years. You just know. All of the hosts and listeners were amazed, but I was covered in hot soup!

All of those listening, including Shawn, had a big laugh over that one. Remember, instant karma is very soon, if not actually instant.

AS WE INCREASE OUR AWARENESS DO WE MOVE OUT OF THE NEED FOR KARMA?

Karma is a Divine system. Whether you think you need it or not, karma "is." Will there ever be no karma? No. If you are in the 3D world, you are subject to karma, and that is how it is. There are two types. Regular karma, as generated in the 1-9 group; or instant karma that the Master vibrations are subject to. We have just covered that again in the last chapter.

You do not move to a higher vibration without what? How do you move from an 8 level to a 9 level? Karma. When you balance all karma in an 8 life path, then and only then, do you proceed and move up to the 9 level. Karma, incurred and balanced, is what moves you to a higher vibration. Darkness from you was balanced by light from the Creator. It was brought through you, the soul. Every time this happens you grow spiritually. You vibrate faster, grow larger, and have become more aware. The darkness stimulates the light. Again, darkness is created first through (or by) the ego (mind) which is its purpose. Light is then brought to that darkness (by the soul) to keep the creation (you) in balance. Darkness is always first.

The Creator commanded light to shine out of darkness. He did not command darkness to shine out of light. You are the darkness and you are the light, just as the Creator is the darkness and the light. The Creator is speaking in the first person in Isaiah 45:7 - "I am the light and I am the dark. I make peace and I create evil." You, being in him and of him, are also darkness and light. It can be no other way.

KARMA FREE BUT STILL SUBJECT TO KARMA

So you never get away from karma, but you get to the point where you have no karma on your books. In finishing the cycle of incarnations at the end of the 9 level, you are karma free and all has been balanced. Your purpose for incarnating has been achieved. You have become and earned the necessary light to ascend or return. You have created yourself above through the flesh below. You have finished the cycle of incarnations, and now you must make a choice. Ascend and return as a new you, or continue your incarnations, also as a new you, with the power and glory that you have earned as a direct servant of the Creator.

If you return to incarnate in service to humanity, then you are subject to instant karma. There are different rules and also more awareness of those rules. But you still incur and clear karma; because nobody can be in a physical body, with an ego that needs to ascend through darkness, and not be increasing through trespassing.

As long as you are in the flesh, the ego/mind insures that you will be incurring darkness. The soul also ensures that you will bring light to this darkness. Again, each time this happens you grow, and so does the entire creation. If the small parts grow, the entire lump grows. The scriptures also verify this.

Romans 11:16 – "If the first fruit (you) are holy, the lump is also holy. And if the root is holy, so are the branches."

Isaiah 37:31 – "They will take root below (on Earth) and bear fruit above (in the Celestial)."

Remember, it is the ego's purpose to trespass or create darkness. It can be no other way. Even great egos that are loved, like Alfie (Allfaaraa's ego), even he trespasses, and we pay the price for it. In fact, Alfie trespasses against his students all the time. I constantly trespass against all that I come in contact with. Alfie is a master of the mental trespass. He has actually invented ways to trespass that were unheard of above or below, and he teaches them both to Angels and demons. These new ways to trespass create instant darkness (and instant light) without a major effect on the trespasser and trespassee. Well, Alfie calls the side effects "butthurtism." By the way, Alfie has used, and still uses, this method on the students on the website all the time. He increases and they increase, and those watching from above and below learn!

Once again, as I said earlier, in any coming together one of three things takes place. Light and light are exchanged, light and dark are exchanged, or dark and dark are exchanged. Every single time two people come together, this happens. It happens in every conversation and in the thought processes that occur afterward also.

CRAFTY EGOS

Understand that the flesh body is usually the victim in the playing out of karma. It suffers the pain and anguish of the trespass. Your ego is very, very crafty. It has no rules in how it creates darkness, and yet it is subject to cause and effect. All great egos realize that they bring the pain on themselves (your/their body) through trespasses. But this is how they (you) grow.

Crafty demons (egos) know that the solution is to be able to create darkness without suffering physical pain in the flesh body. Alfie is the master of the mental trespass that creates an equal (or lesser in most cases) mental trespass from every person he comes in contact with; whether they are an associate, a student, a partner, or a cashier at the corner store. Alfie earns and clears karma through each relationship he has established. Most of the balancing is mental for mental, word for word, or word play, as Alfie calls it. Without the other party even realizing that Alfie has just pushed their buttons, they push back, and both are grown in darkness and light.

This is done through word exchange. However, the other ego/person, never realizing what has just happened to them, only gets angry and thinks Alfie is a jerk. The person responds accordingly. This is the verbal trespass caused and affected in one action instantaneously. We've repeated it several times but, once again, understand that in any coming together of parties, three things can happen.

1) Light and darkness are exchanged and both parties grow.
2) Light and light are exchanged and both parties grow.
3) Darkness and darkness are exchanged and both parties actually grow even more.

For example, Alfie may say to Clarky (Shawn's ego), "So I see you have done nothing as usual today, huh?" This is a verbal trespass elicited to invoke a response from Clarky. The darkness (response) will then come back from Clarky as,

"Dude, you are a jerk. I have been working all day." The words are returned in anger and there is no love in them. Darkness, in the form of drama, has now been increased through Alfie, and now also Shawn as he is sucked into Alfie's game.

Depending on whether Alfie feels that enough darkness has been generated for the growth of Shawn and himself through that exchange of trespasses, he will then bring light to that darkness or continue on with the game. He will then smooth it over by saying, "Ok, just checking" or "Good job." This soothes the feelings of the injured demon with...light. Know that words and thoughts hold great power. Correct usage of them, spiritually, is a key to your ascension.

However, this is a very complicated process and most younger souls/egos do not realize that they have just been increased by the encounter. The after effects of the encounter create a new cause as the ego brings up to the brain the memories of the encounter. These, in turn, can create a new cause through anger from the encounter. Usually, when this happens, the next person that you come in contact with had better look out.

BRING THE LOVE

The key is soothing the cause with the effect, which is bringing light to that darkness. Alfie will bring the love and light to the darkness he has just created. For example, "Of course, I know that you were working very hard all day. You work hard every day in service to humanity, and I know that it isn't easy for you. You are a great servant to the Creator and a gift to humanity, etc." Sometimes Alfie lays it on thick and Clarky has no option but to respond in kind, as love and light attract love and light. You cannot hate on someone who is bringing the love. Know this!

The entire situation may take 3 minutes. In these 3 minutes, darkness has been increased through the two vessels and light has balanced that darkness. Both have gained. Alfie does this on purpose all the time. Most all of humanity does the same thing now. This same scenario plays out in your relationships, friends, family, and you don't know why you do it. But it always happens, do you see?

Your egos may now be saying, "That is stupid. That little bit of drama can grow me and God?!?" Well, if it is so stupid, then after examining yourself, tell me why you continue to do it! And you don't even know you are doing it. Well, until now anyway. It is the play between light and darkness that grows the creation (you).

Proverbs 27:17 – "As iron sharpens iron, so one man sharpens another."

This is exactly what I have been explaining to you. You are refined or sharpened through your relationships. Man refines man.

But no, you cannot be out of the karmic system. It is a 3D system and required in the 3D world.

CAN YOU CLEAR KARMA THROUGH GRACE?

First, let me tell you what grace is. And, by the way, the correct term is "providence," but we'll use "grace" for this discussion.

The religious understanding is that grace is unmerited or undeserved forgiveness from the Creator. However, the Bible says that grace is measured, determined, and dispensed in equal amount to the amount of spirit. The religious have incorrectly arrived at the "unmerited forgiveness" stuff. The Scriptures disagree. Here is the verse:

Ephesians 4:7 – "Every one of us has been given grace according to the measure of the gift of Christ (spirit)."

So the more awareness (light/spirit) that you have, the more grace (forgiveness) that you have.

GRACE IS EARNED

Understand that light or spirit within you has been *earned*. It is earned through incarnation. Through each incarnation you gain in light or spirit. Grace or forgiveness is measured equally to the amount of spirit/light that you have attained. Reread the parable that I laid out earlier from Matthew 25:14. Those that produced more also received more. I also showed how the Creator plays favorites. Your favoritism, or grace, is earned through your work. Your work is to grow the light or spirit. The better you do, the more the Creator does for you. You are the one who decides what you will do, what you will become, and when.

Let us get it down to nuts and bolts. The better the servant you are, and the more you serve the Creator, the more forgiveness he gives you. I have more forgiveness than Shawn does, Shawn may have more forgiveness than another one does.

Do you understand that grace is earned and matched equal to spirit? God's business is spirit. Your job is, through the flesh body, to grow that spirit by growing yourself, the soul and the ego. The spirit is given for profit, which we have said and the Scriptures state. The flesh body is the house or vehicle. You are not the house. You are the occupant of the house. With each incarnation you are moved into a new house, a bigger and better house, with a larger "garage" to store more light. That house is the flesh body.

Let's look at the parable in Matthew – "To one he gave ten, to one he gave five, to one he gave three and to one he gave one." The worker that was given ten measures, he returned ten more when Christ came back to collect, and Christ made him a master of many. That is grace. The one who had five returned five more back, and Christ made him a master of some. That is an example of grace. They are rewarded for doing their job. Again, the spirit is given for profit. Your job is to increase what you were given in the beginning when you first began to incarnate.

Grace is measured to the amount of the spirit within you. More Christ (spirit), more grace. As you grow in spirit (yourself) you earn grace also. Grace is earned forgiveness.

IT'S LIKE A BUSINESS

To the worker that didn't give him back anything (except his original measure of spirit), not only did he not receive any grace, but Christ took away everything that he had, spirit and soul, and gave it to the worker that increased the measure ten times. It is just like a business. Essentially he was fired and all his benefits were taken away.

The Creator's best employees get more favors, more forgiveness, and more grace than his worst employees. It's the same with children. I hate to say it, but if you have children you know that not all of them are loved equally. Those that you love more get more grace, and I know you that have children are all saying, "Oh my god he is right." Those that you love more you give more forgiveness to.

The better the servant, the more forgiveness, and the more you can get away with. Since you and the Creator are one, the more of him in you, the more he is forgiving himself (you).

Believe me, I have been given so much grace through so many lifetimes that I could not even begin to tell you. And I have gotten away with so many punishable acts that even I'm surprised. But I must be one heck of a servant up there, because I have done some crazy stuff and been forgiven for it. Yet I have paid the karmic price required. However, I felt that the instant karma required to balance was much less than normally deserved or required. Remember, no one is out of the system.

Understand that in balancing karma, you are balancing darkness, overcoming darkness. And through this you earn grace!

Karma actually earns you grace. The more karma you create and clear, the more grace you receive. Why? Because clearing karma has done what? It has increased what? It has grown you and increased your Spirit. And who else's Spirit? God's.

So the more karma you clear, the more you increase in spirit, and the better the servant that you are. Grace is given to you because of clearing karma; in other words, by overcoming.

Revelations – "To those who overcome...I will give."

The verse above says it all! Overcoming is what you are doing. Each of you is overcoming the darkness that you create for yourself.

Just as the Scriptures state in Ephesians 4:7 – "But unto every one of us is given *grace* according to the measure of the gift of Spirit/Christ." The more spirit you have, the more grace you have or are given. The measure of Spirit/Christ in you equals the measure of grace that you receive.

WHEN WE BECOME A WORLD KARMA SERVER ARE WE CLEARING THE KARMA OF OTHER BEINGS?

No. No being actually clears another being's karma. You do it yourself and they do it for themselves. You could actually be increasing the karma of others. You are played against each other to both balance and increase. Remember what actually balances and where it comes from.

As a world karma server, you will increase world karma or decrease world karma. But the answer is no. You do not clear anyone's karma for them. However, you will serve the darkness to increase it or serve the light to increase it, by helping to maintain balance of the overall creation in a faster manner. Creation functions through balance and imbalance.

When the creation (world) becomes imbalanced to one side or another, the entire creation of God comes to a halt, since balance is required to ensure growth. The system requires balance between light and dark, yet balance is not always achieved immediately.

World karma servers are used to correct the imbalance of the entire creation by taking on great measures of darkness or light, and transmuting it through their flesh bodies. This is the greatest act of love and compassion for humanity and the Creator possible in this realm. In so doing you are putting your flesh body at risk. You, at the Creator's will,

will be subject to greater evil than can be comprehended. It will be stored in your body for transmutation. You could also be subject to great, great light to be stored within, and then subject to tremendous darkness to balance it.

Can you possibly imagine? You risk your flesh body every moment of every day in service, and thereby risking your very soul and ego. However, once again, you know that no power of an Earthly nature can stand against you. You are an Angel of God, and you rest nestled under the wing of Michael.

Psalm 57:1 – "For in you my soul takes refuge in the shadow of your wings."

Psalm 61:4 – "I long to dwell in your tent forever and take refuge in the shelter of your wings."

In serving others you are served. In giving, you are forgiven. Become the instrument of his peace. Christ was a world karma server that became. He carried the world's sins...darkness and light...transmuting all. Here, again, is one of the few prayers that I recommend:

The Prayer of St. Francis

Lord, make me the instrument of your peace.
Where there is hatred, let me sow love;
Where there is injury, pardon;
Where there is doubt, faith;
Where there is despair, hope;
Where there is darkness, light;
And where there is sadness, joy.

O Divine Master, grant that I may not so much seek
To be consoled as to console;
To be understood as to understand;
To be loved as to love.
For it is in giving that we receive;
It is in forgiving that we are forgiven;
And it is in dying that we are born to eternal life. Amen

Simply stated, choose to lose.

YOU ARE THE TRANSFORMERS

What happens next? Where does all of the darkness and light that we have created go? How does it benefit us? Is there a purpose to all of the pain that we must endure in a physical flesh body?

Let me further explain what we are doing here in this world.

Matter is energy waiting to transform. Spirit is matter that has already transformed. Matter is energy waiting to become light or spirit. Spirit transforms matter/darkness into spirit/light. You are the transformers. You are actually transforming matter/darkness into spirit/light through the flesh body. This is what you do. This is the lofty task for which you have been called. You are creating the Creator!

You begin as a small seed, planted in the soil, the flesh body, and through each incarnation you bring light to darkness, or spirit to matter. As you do this you transform your flesh body genetically and spiritually to increase the amount of light that the body can hold, and in so doing you grow spiritually and so does the Creator.

This entire 3D world was created to grow or increase light/spirit through darkness, or to transform matter into light/spirit. This is done through each incarnation. As you bring light from above into matter or flesh, this mixture of darkness and light (the creation) cannot be stored in your flesh body for any length of time. When the container (your body) is filled, it must be emptied in order to be refilled again. This happens over and over throughout the lifetime.

The body begins as an empty container. When it is filled, the mixture of darkness and light is then carried upward and placed in your Astral body in the Astral realm, where it continues the refining process. There are nine levels in the Astral that line up with the nine levels of incarnation. The physical body is actually a mini refinement, or purification, center used to transform darkness into light, step by step. The Astral realm is a gigantic holding center for the spiritual matter or material that you and all incarnate supply.

As an analogy, the flesh body is an empty glass of water. You, the ego, fill it with dark water and then you, the soul, fill it with light water. Over and over, you fill it with dark water and then fill it with light water, always keeping it in balance. When the glass gets full the contents are moved to the Astral, to a larger holding facility, as "you." The light water has transformed the dark water, which we call the "mixture," since they have been mixed together. It is also *more* than it was. It began as an empty glass, but now you have filled it with (created) a mixture of light and dark, which are both aspects of the Creator. Hence you have increased him and yourself.

Each time the body is filled and emptied it is increased in size, like a balloon, and is able to carry more light and more darkness. You modify you. In your next incarnation that mixture will be further refined. The mixture you create is like wine, it gets better as it ages. The Creator adds "leaven" (his Holy Spirit) to the entire lump (Astral) to increase the process.

1 Corinthians 5:6 – "Know you not that a little leaven leavens the whole lump."

The whole cycle happens all over again in the next incarnation. Except that this time you start out with what you previously created, instead of nothing. The new mixture, which you created in the previous incarnation and stored in the Astral, is again placed into your flesh body. Dark is again brought to light, and the resulting mixture (further refined) is again placed in the Astral on your account, so to speak. This is done on a continuous basis during the lifetime, as the body is filled and emptied, filled and emptied, over and over.

You began with nothing, an empty glass or vessel. However, by your third incarnation in the flesh, you have created a mixture of spirit and matter, or light and darkness, and have at minimum tripled the size and quality of yourself. As we have said again and again (because it is important) you create yourself and thereby the Creator also. With each incarnation the mixture becomes more light based than it is dark based, and it is refined to an even greater level while it sits in the larger refinement tank in the Astral realm. The whole creation (lump) is refined or "leavened" as it is stored in the Astral.

YOU ARE THE BUILDERS

You have to understand how important you are and how important the 3D body that you have is. You grow the universe, every one of you. You are the builders of all universes. You transform matter into spirit, by bringing light to darkness. And you transform spirit back into matter when you come back to incarnate. Your 3D body is created from the material or mixture that you have supplied. It is transformed back into the matter that makes up your physical body.

Science will tell you that the universe is expanding. Thus said, where do you think the material comes from to increase the universe? Is there a matter factory or what? The answer is yes. This world is the supplier of spiritual material, the mixture of dark and light, matter and spirit created through your flesh body. This is what the Creator uses to increase himself and thereby all of creation. You produce and grow the material that the Creator uses to extend the universes, including all worlds, aliens, E.T.'s, and every realm. You are the producers! Let me bow to the great service that everyone of you does. But none of you know it, not any of you, although some of you might have an idea.

IMAGINE IF EVERYONE KNEW

Imagine if you really knew the truth of how important you are? What if humanity knew? What if everyone knew why they are here and how important it is to creation as a whole? Would you then see that we are all one, with a single purpose?

YOUR LOFTY TASK

Creating yourself above, and thereby God and the universes, through incarnating in the flesh below. Bringing your entire Angel or I AM Presence into form. This is the lofty task for which you came. You are the builders of all universes. The service that you perform is for all life forms. You are growing all worlds, *including your very own.* Everything that you provide is used by the Creator to create new universes, including your own universe!

THE COPTIC PSALM BOOK

As I am editing this and getting ready for our weekly radio show, I decided to pick up "The Other Bible." Flipping through it I came to a book called "The Coptic Psalm Book." Understand that I don't read books for any of my understandings. I am taught directly by both Michael/Christ and Lucifer. First they teach, and if I question, then they prove it by directing me to find the teaching in print. Most everything I teach is proven through the Scriptures, including the Dead Sea Scrolls, the Nag Hammadi, the Gnostic Gospels, the Bible, and even the Urantia Book.

After preparing this teaching for the radio show, I came to The Coptic Psalm Book and was astounded at what I saw. In hearing what I have laid out above, some of you may be a little overwhelmed, or maybe in doubt.

This is for you.

Again, this teaching came directly to me from above four years *before* the written verification from The Coptic Psalm Book. Here it is in print:

"When the first man (Lucifer) had ended his struggle, the Father sent his second son (Michael). He came and helped his brother out of the abyss. He (Michael) built this whole world up out of the mixture that had come into existence out of light and darkness. The world is also, however, a

place for purification for the soul, which had been swallowed up in the powers of darkness. The Sun (Michael) and the Moon (Lucifer) were set up and fixed in the heights to purify the soul. They take the refined material (mixture) upward daily to the heights (Astral). They convey it up and down."

What are they carrying up and down? You!!!

As Christ says in the Gospel of Thomas, when you first understand this you will become troubled and then astonished.

This should supply some additional reinforcement to what I have just disclosed to you. That you supply the mixture of darkness and light that the Creator uses to build worlds! This includes your own world, directly created from the mixture of light and dark that you supply!

You are the builders. Take a bow my lofty ones!

"The path of light is laid, the sacred test.
Let Angels guide you on your lofty quest."
Milton, Paradise Lost

EPILOGUE

To those of you that have finished this book I say this:
I know that we were unable to cover every single aspect and
every occurrence that can possibly be. If after purchasing
this book you have questions, you may ask them on the
website and I will personally answer them. What hopefully
you have come to understand from this information is:

That your primary purpose for being incarnate in this world
is to grow the Creator through growing yourself.

That karma is a Divine system that guarantees that most all
will return or ascend.

That you are the master of your own karma.
That you incur it and you remove it.

That both you the ego and you the soul have opposite
purposes, yet both purposes align so that both work
together to ensure your ascension.

That you are the evil.
That you are also the good.

The greater the darkness,
The greater the light.

Your spiritual growth comes through overcoming the
darkness that you have created.

Your light (spirit) within grows through darkness.

Karma is the Divine system that keeps the entire creation in balance.

You are the God of your own karma.

Karma brings order out of chaos.
Light out of darkness.
And guarantees the one predetermined thing in this world.
That the Creator will grow as you are grown, through the incurring and balancing of your karma.

1 Corinthians 15:43 & 44
It (seed/soul) is sown in dishonor (flesh),
It is raised in glory (spirit).
It is sown in weakness,
It is raised in power.
It (soul/seed) is sown in a natural body,
It is raised in a spiritual body.
There is a natural body and there is a spiritual body.

49 And as we (seeds/souls/you) have borne the image of the Earthly (flesh) we shall also bear the image of the Heavenly (Angels).

God is all there is.
There is nothing he is not.
He is every molecule and particle of everything that exists in this created world as well as the multi-universal creations.

In growing any aspect of the creation,
The entire creation (God) grows.

He is the good and the evil, the light and the dark.
No matter which is grown, he grows.

Isaiah 45:7 (KJV)
I AM THE LIGHT
AND I AM THE DARK
I MAKE PEACE AND
I CREATE EVIL

* * *

~ I AM ALLFAARAA ANTAARAA AMAARAA ~

THANK YOU ~ THANK YOU ~ THANK YOU

* * *